SOUL

& Spirit

SOUL

& Spirit

By Edgar Cayce

ARE
PRESS

ASSOCIATION FOR
RESEARCH AND
ENLIGHTENMENT

A.R.E. Press • Virginia Beach • Virginia

A.R.E. Press
215 67th Street
Virginia Beach, VA 23451-2061

Cayce, Edgar, 1877-1945.
   Soul and spirit / by Edgar Cayce
      p.   cm.
   ISBN-10   0-87604-550-6 (trade pbk.)
   ISBN-13   978-0-87604-550-3 (trade pbk.)
      1. Parapsychology–Religious aspects. 2. Spirituality. 3. Soul. 4. Spirit.
I. Title. II. Title: Soul and spirit.
   BF1040.C39 2006
   133.8—dc22

                                    2006023467

Cover design by Richard Boyle

Contents

Foreword
Who Was Edgar Cayce?

It is a time in the earth when people everywhere seek to know more of the mysteries of the mind, the soul," said my grandfather, Edgar Cayce, from an unconscious trance from which he demonstrated a remarkable gift for clairvoyance.

His words are prophetic even today, as more and more Americans in these unsettled times are turning to psychic explanations for daily events. For example, according to a survey by the National Opinion Research Council nearly half of American adults believe they have been in contact with someone who has died, a figure twice that of ten years earlier. Two-thirds of all adults say they have had an ESP experience; ten years before that figure was only one-half.

Every culture throughout history has made note of its own members' gifted powers beyond the five senses. These rare individuals held special interest because they seemed able to provide solutions to life's pressing problems. America in the twenty-first century is no exception.

Edgar Cayce was perhaps the most famous and most carefully documented psychic of our time. He began to use his unusual abilities when he was a young man, and from then on for over forty years he would, usually twice a day, lie on a couch, go into a sleeplike state, and respond to questions. Over fourteen thousand of these discourses, called readings, were carefully transcribed by his secretary and preserved by the Edgar Cayce Foundation in Virginia Beach, Virginia. These psychic readings continue to provide inspiration, insight, and help with healing to tens of thousands of people.

Having only an eighth-grade education, Edgar Cayce lived a plain and simple life by the world's standards. As early as his childhood in Hopkinsville, Kentucky, however, he sensed that he had psychic ability. While alone one day he had a vision of a woman who told him he would have unusual power to help people. He also related experiences of "seeing" dead relatives. Once, while struggling with school lessons, he slept on his spelling book and awakened knowing the entire contents of the book.

As a young man he experimented with hypnosis to treat a recurring throat problem that caused him to lose his speech. He discovered that under hypnosis he could diagnose and describe treatments for the physical ailments of others, often without knowing or seeing the person with the ailment. People began to ask him other sorts of questions, and he found himself able to answer these as well.

In 1910 the *New York Times* published a two-page story with pictures about Edgar Cayce's psychic ability as described by a young physician, Wesley Ketchum, to a clinical research society in Boston. From that time on people from all over the country with every conceivable question sought his help.

In addition to his unusual talents, Cayce was a deeply religious man who taught Sunday school all of his adult life and read the entire Bible once for every year that he lived. He always tried to attune himself to God's will by studying the Scriptures and maintaining a rich prayer life, as well as by trying to be of service to those who came seeking help. He used his talents only for helpful purposes. Cayce's simplicity and humility and his commitment to doing good in the world continue to attract people to the story of his life and work and to the far-reaching information he gave.

Charles Thomas Cayce, Ph.D.
Executive Director
Association for Research and Enlightenment, Inc.

Editor's Explanation of Cayce's Discourses

Edgar Cayce dictated all of his discourses from a self-induced trance. A stenographer took his discourses down in shorthand and later typed them. Copies were sent to the person or persons who had requested the psychic reading, and one was put into the files of the organization, which built up around Cayce over the years, the Association for Research and Enlightenment (better known as the A.R.E.).

In his normal consciousness, Edgar Cayce spoke with a Southern accent but in the same manner as any other American. However, from the trance state, he spoke in the manner of the King James Bible, using "thees" and "thous." In trance, his syntax was also unusual. He put phrases, clauses, and sentences together in a manner that slows down any reader and requires careful attention in order to be sure of his meaning. This caused his stenographer to adopt some unusual punctuation in order to put into sentence form some of the long, complex thoughts conveyed by Cayce while in trance. Also, many of his discourses are so jam-packed with information and insights that it requires that one slow down and read more carefully in order to fully understand what he is intending.

From his trance state, Cayce explained that he got his information from two sources: (1) the inquiring individual's mind, mostly from his or her deeper, subconscious mind and (2) from the Universal Consciousness, the infinite mind within which the entire universe is conscious. He explained that every action and thought of every individual makes an impression upon the Universal Consciousness, an impression that can be psychically read. He correlated this with the Hindu concept of an Akashic Record, which is an ethereal, fourth-dimensional film upon which actions and thoughts are recorded and can be read at any time.

When giving one of his famous health readings, called physical readings, Cayce acted as if he were actually scanning the entire body of the person, from the inside out! He explained that the subconscious mind of everyone contains all of the data on the condition of the physical body it inhabits, and Cayce simply connected with the patient's deeper mind. He could also give the cause of the condition, even if it was from early childhood or from many lifetimes ago in a previous incarnation of the soul. This was knowable because the soul remembers all of its experiences. He explained that deeper portions of the subconscious mind are the mind of the soul, and portions of the subconscious and the soul are in the body with the personality.

In life readings and topic readings, Cayce also connected with the subconscious minds of those inquiring as well as the Universal Consciousness.

Occasionally, Cayce would not have the material being requested, and he would say, "We do not have that here." This implied that Cayce's mind was more directed than one might think. He was not open to everything. From trance, he explained that the suggestion given at the beginning of one of his psychic readings so directed his deeper mind and focused it on the task or subject requested that he truly did not have other topics available. However, on a few occasions, he seemed able to shift topics in the middle of a reading.

The typed readings have a standard format. Numbers were used in the place of the name of the person or persons receiving the reading, and a dash system kept track of how many readings the person had received. For example, reading 137-5 was the fifth reading for Mr. [137]. In most cases, only a paragraph or two of a reading were pertinent to our study, and then I only give the reading number. If a complete reading is used, the reading number, the date and location, and the names or numbers (for privacy) of those in attendance are given. Occasionally the stenographer would include a note about other conditions, such as the presence of a manuscript that the in-trance Cayce was supposed to view psychically and comment on. As I explained, Cayce dictated all of these discourses while he was in trance. In most cases, he spoke in a monotone voice. However, he would sometimes elevate his volume when saying a word or phrase. In these instances, his stenographer usually typed these words with all-capital letters, to give the reader some sense of Cayce's increased volume. These all-capital letters have been changed to italic typeface for readability, as well as emphasis. In many cases, these words appear to be rightly accentuated in Cayce's discourses. However, in some cases, it is not clear why he raised his voice.

Another style that the stenographer adopted was to capitalize all of the letters in Cayce's many affirmations (positive-thought or prayer-like passages to be used by the recipient as a tool for focusing and/or raising consciousness). I have also changed these to upper- and lower-case letters and italicized them. Questions asked Cayce have also been italicized for easier reference.

Whenever his stenographer was not sure if she had written down the correct word or thought that she might have missed or misunderstood a word, she inserted suggested words, comments, and explanations in [brackets]. If she knew of another reading that had similar material or that was being referred to during this reading, she would put the reading number in brackets. Cayce's entire collection of readings is available on CD-ROM from the A.R.E., so, even though the referenced reading may not be in this book, I left these references in for any future research; but several of the readings that have references are in this book. Within the text of a reading, all (parentheses) are asides made by Cayce himself while in trance, not by his stenographer. She only used [brackets] within the text of a reading. In the preliminary material, she used parentheses in the normal manner. My comments are indicated by the term "Editor's Note."

A few common abbreviations used in these discourses were: "GD" for Gladys Davis, the primary stenographer; "GC" for Gertrude Cayce, Edgar's wife and the predominant conductor of the readings; "HLC" for Hugh Lynn Cayce; and "EC" for Edgar Cayce.

—John Van Auken, Editor

1

●

Spirit

Reading 816–10

Spirit is the natural, the normal condition of an entity. For hath it not been given, God is Spirit and seeketh such to worship Him, in spirit and in truth?

And then, as must be seen, must be felt, must be experienced sooner or later the awareness, the consciousness that, only *spirit* is everlasting, then the promptings, the balance must be spiritual in its essence in dealing with or judging the mental attitudes, the social relationships, the material experiences.

Reading 262–123

(Q) *Give a definition of Spirit which may be given in the lesson.*

(A) Spirit is the First Cause, the primary beginning, the motivative influence—as God is Spirit.

Reading 2533–1

There may be the greater expression materially of mental and spiritual aspects of each soul. While body is subject to all the influences of materiality, it may be controlled—the emotions thereof—by the mind. And the mind may be directed by spirit. Spirit is that portion of the First Cause which finds expression in all that is everlasting in the consciousness of mind *or* matter.

Reading 900-16

(Q) *Explain the various planes of eternity, in their order of development, or rather explain to us the steps through which the soul must pass to climb back into the arms of beloved God.*

(A) These, we see, must be manifest only as the finite mind in the flesh. As in the spirit forces, the development comes through the many changes, as made manifest in the evolution of man.

In the development in eternity's realm, is that a finite force as made of creation may become one with the Creator, as a unit, atom, or vibration, becomes one with the universal forces. When separated, as each were in the beginning, with the many changes possible in the material forces, the development then comes, that each spirit entity, each earth entity, the counterpart of the spirit entity, may become one with the Creator, even as the ensample to man's development through flesh, made perfect in every manner; though taking on flesh, yet without spot or blemish, never condemning, never finding fault, never bringing accusation against any, making the will one with the Father, as was in the beginning. For, without passing through each and every stage of development, there is not the correct vibration to become one with the Creator, beginning with the first vibration, as is of the spirit quickened with the flesh, and made manifest in material world (earth's plane).

Then, in the many stages of development, throughout the universal, or in the great system of the universal forces, and each stage of development made manifest through flesh, which is the testing portion of the universal vibration. In this manner then, and for this reason, all made manifest in flesh, and development, through the eons of time, space, and *called* eternity.

(Q) *What is this spirit entity in the body, [900], and how may he develop it in the right direction?*

(A) This is only the portion that develops other than in the earth's plane. Spirit entity. For soul's development is in the earth's plane. The spirit entity is in the spirit plane.

(Q) *Does the spirit entity have a separate consciousness apart from the physical, and is it as the consciousness of [900] when he dreams, or has visions, while asleep?*

(A) The spirit entity is a thing apart from any earthly connection in sleep, yet connected. For the earthly or material consciousness is ever tempered with material conditions; the superconsciousness with the consciousness between soul and spirit, and partakes of the spiritual forces principally. In consciousness we find only projections of subconscious and superconscious, which conditions project themselves in dreams, visions, unless entered into the superconscious forces. In the consciousness of earthly or material forces there enters all the attributes of the physical, fleshly body. In the subconscious there enters the attributes of soul forces, and of the conscious forces. In the superconscious there enters the subconscious forces, and spiritual discernment and development.

Reading 900–24

(Q) Have the lower forms of creation, such as animals, any life in the spirit plane?
(A) All have the spirit force.

A Well-Balanced Ideal
Reading 4866–2

What it [the self] would work toward must have a great deal to do with what may be called an entirely successful operation, an entirely successful development for the body; for what the body sets as its ideal, whether that which is wholly of the material or that which is a well-balanced spiritual, mental and material condition, will be those developments; for the activity—whether of wholly material conditions, mental conditions, or of spiritual conditions—is the *spirit* with which an entity, a body, goes about its activity. If the life is to become wholly mechanical, or wholly material minded, then only the material will be the natural result, and this will *not* bring contentment—nor will it satisfy. If the ideal will be set as a well-balanced self, knowing that the spirit, the life—that is, the spirit *is* the life, the mental attitude is the development or the builder—then the results will be in that comparison as to the activity that is given in respect to these attitudes.

Seat of the Soul and Spirit in the Body
Reading 4595-1
The sympathetic forces [are] the seat of all of the soul and spirit forces [in the physical body].

Editor's Note: The sympathetic nervous system includes the seven endocrine glands, which other Cayce readings identify as the physical portions of the seven chakras.

The Spirit and Soul Are Naturally Psychic
Reading 3744-2
(Q) *Please give a definition of psychic phenomena.*

(A) *Psychic* means of the *Spirit* or *Soul*, for cooperation of the Phenomena, or manifestation of the workings of those forces within the individual, or through the individual, from whom such phenomena, or of such phases of the working of the spirit and soul, to bring the actions of these to the physical plane, Phenomena meaning only the act itself, brought to the attention, or manifested in such a way as to bring the attention of an individual to the work itself.

Psychic in the broader sense meaning spirit, soul, or the imagination of the mind, when attuned to the various phases of either of these two portions of the entity of an individual, or from the entity of others who are passed into the other planes than the physical or material; yet in the broader sense, the Phenomena of Psychic forces is as material as the forces that become visible to the material or physical plane.

Psychic forces cover many various conditions, depending upon the development of the individual, or how far distant the entity is from the plane of spirit and soul forces.

Psychic means not understood from the physical, or material, or conscious mind.

Psychic means that of the mind presenting the soul and the spirit entity as manifested in the individual mind. Then taking the phases of that force, we find all Psychic Phenomena or force, presented through one of the acknowledged five senses of the physical or material body— these being used as the mode of manifesting to individuals. Hence we would have in the truest sense, *psychic*, meaning the expression to the material world of the latent, or hidden sense of the soul and spirit forces, whether manifested from behind, or in and through the material plane.

The Difference Between Soul Forces and Spirit
Reading 900-17

(Q) It has been given that the soul is the spiritual force that animates or gives life to the body. What is spirit? What is spiritual force? Is it corporeal or incorporeal? Where may we find the soul force in the body—in the brain, nerve centers or where?

(A) There is a vast deal of difference between spiritual and soul forces, for, as given, each force there has been set guards or bounds. Spirit forces are the animation of *all life* giving life–producing forces in animate or inanimate forces. Spiritual elements become corporeal when we speak of the spiritual body in a spiritual entity; then composed of spirit, soul and the superconsciousness.

In the soul forces, and its dwelling in man, we find the animation, the spiritual element, the soul that developing element, and contained in the brain, in the nerve, in the centers of the whole system. As to the specific centers, nearer those centers of the sensory system, physically speaking.

In the conditions, then, we find when soul and spirit take flight from the animate forces of an human, we find the deadening of all the centers of the sensory system, with the vitality of the solar plexus system, with the gland of the medulla oblongata, these then controlling the forces, and the life becomes extinct, with soul and spirit, with the superconscious forces, gone.

Then, we have as this:

Spiritual element, the vitality, produces the motive forces of the entity, whether physical or spiritual. Spiritual forces being the life, the reproductive principle; the soul the development principle. As we have manifested, or illustrated, in the physical body in nerve tissue: There becomes that principle of the nerve action and the nerve in action. That is, with the expression of some condition bringing distress in the body, the active principle is the spirit. The nerve is the soul, for development.

(Q) What happens to the conscious mind forces and physical forces at death?

(A) The conscious mind forces either are in the soul's development, and in the superconsciousness, or left with that portion of material forces which goes to the reclaiming, or remoulding, of physical bodies, for indwelling of spiritual entities.

With What Spirit You Act . . .

Reading 257–238

(Q) Did I conduct myself properly with the people I have met so far at the War Department?

(A) We do not find fault, but this of course should be determined by self—rather than from other sources. Remember, these conditions exist, and keep this ever before thee: The real intent and purpose in declarations call from the spiritual forces that influence which is for good or bad. That, to be sure, is free will. Hence the injunctions as have been so oft given the body—do not appear to be that ye really are not. Be sincere with self and ye will not be false or insincere with others. The spirit of truth brings the outward appearance of that desire first suggested, if the body and mind are in keeping with that as would be pleasing to the influences or forces called God. For, the declaration of each soul sets in motion that spirit. What spirit do ye entertain? Truth, justice, mercy, love, patience, brotherly kindness? Or self, self–praise, self–glory that ye may be wellspoken of materially? These choices are made by the individual. Their results, their effects in the lives of individuals are such as to determine spiritual success, material success, or a well–rounded mental, spiritual *and* material success. For, the earth is the Lord's and the fulness thereof. The abilities that have been lent thee, keep inviolate—if ye would be in keeping with His purposes with thee.

Thou hast the ability to bring truth and light to many. These are then within thine own keeping, according to the manner in which ye conduct thyself before others. With what spirit, with what purpose do ye serve?

Greater Joy

Reading 816–3

Much of that the entity has thought, has experienced, is cherished more from within. Yet, if there were some changes in these directions, there may be a greater joy in the living in this experience. For while that sojourn gives those influences which make for abilities in being able to cope with conditions and experiences in the lives of individuals and groups and masses, if these are held only in self and not given out with that love of service, for the abilities within self to give expressions of the love of a divine Father, they may become stumblingblocks in thine experience. For all force, all manifestations in materiality are the expressions of spirit, and are *prompted* by same. Are these influences of the divine, or dost thou cherish those that at times may become questioned? Know in what, in whom, thou hast believed, and know whether it be of a constructive or of a growing influence for the spirit of truth or not. For the promise is given to all, "My spirit beareth witness with thy spirit as to whether thou art choosing good or evil in all of thy ways."

Reading 1257–1

Know that the *living* forces of thy God are *active!* Not as of stone or wood but as the spirit of truth that casteth out fear, that bringeth peace, that bringeth harmony, that bringeth those things that make for the associations with thy fellow man as a better neighbor, a better sister, a better daughter, a better mother, a better citizen.

Reading 1265–1

What, then, *is* thine ideal? Is it founded in that ye yourself may do, or that in which ye may be the *channel* through which others may find *their* association with a *living* God, a living ideal, a living love, a living faith, a living experience of joy? *These* be they which are of the truth, and thus grow as does the spirit of truth.

so *is* he! Not what *man* says, nor what man even makes *out* like he does! for we are gradually builded to that image created within our own mental being; for, as has been given, the Spirit is the life, the Mind is the active forces that, coordinated with the spirit that is of the creative energy, or for God, gives the physical result that is effective in every sense. Get that!

Reading 345–2

(Q) How may the entity control same?

(A) Know better that as has been given aforetime. Know that all power, or all force, is an emanation of One Spirit. *Try* each, and see whether these emanations are true and in accord with that as has been given, that "My spirit bear witness with *your* spirit as to whether the truth *is* that making one free, or does such an emanation bind the mental and spiritual body; for remember, as given, the spiritual is the life; the mental is the builder. Were [If] that emanation from the spirit force [were] manifested, one that binds rather than loosens, then this—as seen—would be an incorrect or improper emanation.

Reading 349–4

(Q) What does may horoscope predict for 1928?

(A) That as has been outlined aforetime for the body; though, as has been given, the will and the application of those conditions as present themselves as urges are the results of application of will, irrespective of that as would be given from the horoscope inflection or urge from same. Rather build that within self with the sure knowledge of life, self, body, mind, spended in the proper direction brings that one sows; for be not deceived, God is not mocked, and what a body—mentally, physically, spiritually—sows, that it reaps! and not something else! Wishes do not bring other than desire. Is desire of that that builds in the proper sense, in the proper order with spirit, soul or mind *and* body? for the spirit is life; the mind is the builder; the physical is the result. Guide, keep, self aright.

(Q) Mentally, spiritually and socially?

(A) Physically, mentally, spiritually and socially, by application. Remembering that as has just been given. The mental, the spiritual, are unseen forces; the activities are the result of mental application; physical conditions—whether pertaining to social, to money, to station in life, to likes and dislikes—are the application of those mental images builded within the body, seated, guided, directed, by the spiritual application of that of the spirit within bearing witness within self to the spirit of the universe, or to God, and the forces as are seen are *results! What wilt thou build within thine self!*

Reading 524–2

(Q) *How may the material activities and the spiritual purpose be coordinated?*

(A) That in the material world is a shadow of that in the celestial or spiritual world. Then, the material manifestations of spiritual impulse or activity must be in keeping or in attune with that which has its inception in *spiritual* things. For, the *mind* of man *is* the builder; and if the beginning is in spiritual life, and the mental body sees, acts upon, is motivated only by the spiritual, then the physical result will be in keeping with that thou hast sown. For, what ye sow ye shall reap, and God is not mocked; for the desire, the intent and purpose must be toward that first law as given: "Thou shalt have no other gods before me. Thou shalt love the Lord thy God with all thine heart, thine soul, thine body." If the activities make for the exaltation of the mind, the body, or the position, power, wealth or fame, *these* are of the earth–earthy. Not that there should not be the material things, but the result of spiritual activity—*not* the result of the desires for that which the material things bring *as* power to a soul.

Reading 585–1

(Q) *Did I remember the message correctly, and what was meant by it?*

(A) A warning of those conditions, that there be not a departing from the way in which self has brought self to an understanding, in its present concept of true mental and spiritual relationships; for, as has been given, Michael is the lord of the Way—and in the *ways* of understanding, of conception, of bringing about those things that make for the changes in the attitudes in physical, mental or material relationships, is the *guide* through such spiritual relations; for the spiritual is the life, the light, the mental is the builder, the material and physical are the results of those activities as applied in the material, carnal or physical plane.

Reading 622–6

Thus it becomes each soul—in its realization, in its awareness, in its seeking—to know the Author of its ideal—spiritually, mentally, materially. The spiritual is the life, the mental is the builder, the material is the result of that builded through the purposes held by the individual entity.

Reading 815–3

If there is builded in the mental forces of the body that there is a hindrance, that there is that which cuts self short in any manner, it is gradually builded so that it becomes a barrier to not only the efficiency of the body. But it should be considered by the body that the *sources* of supply are—in their elementals, or in their first premise—*spiritual* in nature; also that the Creative Force (or God) is the motivative force in that which is of an idealistic nature, in whatever form of endeavor the body engages. This is true whether pertaining to the efficient activities as to the psychological effect of advertising upon individuals' minds or as to the correction of those that have attempted to use their own mental forces in depicting the experiences of life in a play or script for advertising forces upon the radio or the like.

Reading 900–10

(Q) As created by God in the first, are souls perfect, and if so, why any need of development?

(A) In this we find only the answer in this: The evolution of life as may be understood by the finite mind. In the first cause, or principle, all is perfect. In the creation of soul, we find the portion may become a living soul and equal with the Creator. To reach that position, when separated, must pass through all stages of development, that it may be one with the Creator. As we have is this:

Man. In the beginning, we find the spirit existent in all living force. When such force becomes inanimate in finite forces [it is] called dead; not necessarily losing its usefulness, either to Creator, or created, in material world. In that of creation of man, we find all the elements in a

living, moving, world, or an element in itself; yet without that experience as of a first cause, yet endowed with all the various modifications
of elements or forces manifested in each. For first there is the spirit, then
soul (man we are speaking of), then mind with its various modifications
and with its various incentives, with its various ramifications, if you
please, and the will the balance in the force that may make all or lose
all.

In the developing, then, that the man may be one with the Father,
necessary that the soul pass, with its companion the will, through all
the various stages of development, until the will is lost in Him and he
becomes one with the Father.

In the illustration of this, we find in the man as called Jesus. In this:
This man, as man, makes the will the will of the Father, then becoming
one with the Father and the model for man.

Reading 900-374

*(Q) While riding one afternoon about February 8th. My hand wandering over
side of car as I reflected upon movie actors seemed to write: "John Drew." I wondered
how I could meet these actors and the thought came to me: "I will direct you." Later in
the Metro-Goldwyn studio I felt the cosmic presence in my keen appreciation of de-
tails of actors' work and its relationship to human nature. I did not see there an
opening to any individually as to be able to interest them in our work. How may this
be done?*

(A) Even as was seen (this material now—for a material application of
a mental and spiritual truth), as was experienced by the entity in making physical application, there is seen or felt the spiritual presence of a
truth to which the mental mind had been directed. In the presence
there is felt that in the action of those before the body was that sincere
desire in the minds and hearts and beings of many to as vividly portray
lessons as the entity itself would give concerning forces, concerning
laws, concerning application of life to the various phenomena of life. In
that found by entity of the inability to approach an individual or a
personality upon the subject, would the entity but consider as to the
laws as have been given, that this *would* be such a circumstance; for first
it must come to an individual, and choosing one whom the entity knows
is inclined or has the appreciation of one or more of the laws, then

physically approach same. *This* manner, this channel, *anyone* that the entity might approach would listen, and little by little there would come that opening wedge through which the seeds of truth may be sown or given. Remembering ever, mental law in mental application; spiritual law in spiritual application; and that *material* conditions are the *outgrowth* of the application of each; for *mind* the builder; the spirit the creator; the material (of which visibility is given) that created. Great truth! Keep it before you.

Reading 903-6

Yes, we have the body here—this we have had before. Now, we find the body very good respecting physical conditions of the body. While there are changes taking place with and for the physical forces, these are of the natural development of conditions as respecting both physical and mental attitude of the body, and there needs be kept that same mental and physical attitude toward the developments that are arising, and will arise in the physical forces of the body, to bring about those normal conditions as have been outlined for the body. This the mental attitude of conditions, and developments are as the growth of the mental development of the body—dependent upon that which the body gives—physically and mentally—to the being dependent upon the body; for, as we find here, there is that full demonstration of how that life projects itself in a mental attitude, and is the continual growth of that projected; for the spiritual forces—which is the life—is as that projected, and that builded is the outcome of the attitude, and mental forces as well as physical of the body. Following those, then, with that same prayerful attitude as is and was attained in that union bringing about those conditions in and for the body. Ready for questions.

Reading 911-2

In considering conditions in the spiritual, it is recognized by the body more and more that all things that have to do with the mental and physical body must of themselves have their inception in the spiritual; else the results, or the fruits of either physical or mental experience, must become more or less blasted by the associations assumed in the application of an idea or ideal in connection or association with individuals, places or peoples, or things. Hence the spiritual is as a criterion for the development of the mental and the spiritual welfare of an individual, and particularly must it mean so to this entity, or individual, as the conditions physical develop, as the outlook opens upon the affairs, conditions, relationships with the body, under the new or different conditions as they develop.

Then, as we find, the body physical is on the improve, and there is less and less dependence upon those outside influences, and more and more does the body depend upon that influence from within and the abilities of the physical to create and maintain those necessary elements in the physical organism for the responses in same to be more and more of self; there will be seen that the physical depends upon the spiritual aspect the body has, and more will the spiritual function as the ideals of the body are held in that position or manner in which the ideal is the guide and the guard to the activities of the mental and material body.

(Q) How often should it be taken?

(A) As the necessity demands that it be taken. As is seen here, there has been the dependence of the system upon the activity of same in reference to the using up of the hydrates and the fats, that there be the proper balance for the carrying forward of all forces necessary in the blood supply for the common functioning of the organs of the system, see? and, as has been given, as the impulses—by the relieving of those pressures in the cerebro-spinal and sympathetic nerve system—allow the organs to become more and more active, then less and less often and less and less quantity will be needed for the activities of the system; until, as has been given, the body has within self that which is capable of adjusting itself; for the basis of the active forces in the body is founded and grounded in the spiritual essence of creative energy within self—or the spiritual.

Reading 912–1

(Q) Any further physical conditions to correct?

(A) As we find, as given, the physical forces of the body are very good. These tendencies in the directions of some of the conditions referred to cause much of the drain upon the system, that makes for those weaknesses in some directions. Keep before the mental body that that will ever be *constructive* in its nature; for the mind *is* the builder, the spiritual or the ideal is the life. If the ideal is set in material things, these do rust, they do corrupt. If the ideal is set in heavenly things, in spiritual things, they grow brighter by use, they grow more harmonious by their age and attunement, and build in the material body, the material experience of the body, that which is *satisfying* in that it brings contentment.

Reading 961–1

As ye sow in spirit, so may the mind build that ye reap in materiality. As ye sow in materiality, so may that mind build to make for dissension or a paralleling of an activity in the spiritual import. They are interchangeable.

Reading 1246–2

(Q) How can my organization—?

(A) As has been indicated, first it's the individual that is in the position that reaches to the masses. Through these. For the laws as given do not string along; they are part one of another—the spiritual, the mental, the material. For that as conceived in spirit, in mental finds expression and growth, and in the material comes into activity.

Reading 1579–1

The spirit is the life. Then each phase of the experience of the entity must be of the spiritual import in its very nature, if it is to live, to be the fulfilling of its purpose—to bring peace and harmony, for which purpose it *is* in existence! It must be constructive in the very nature and the very desires, without thought of self being the one glorified in or by same! Rather the *glory* is to the influence or force that *prompts* same!

Reading 1597–1

For the activity is first in spirit, then in mind, and *then* it may become a *material* manifestation. One is the projection as it were of the other into materialization, as we see about us in the earth.

Reading 1671–2

Hence these are from that premise that the mental and spiritual is that portion that must be the directing force, and that material successes—so called—will be the result of well-applied spiritual and mental purposes and desires by the entity.

For without a knowledge of spiritual and mental things, little of growth or advancement may be made by an entity.

Reading 1710–3

These, to be sure, will be approached more from the spiritual aspects. For, know within self (and these are immutable laws), that which will be helpful, hopeful or eternal must be founded in spirituality, and not merely ideas for self-advancement, self-aggrandizement, or to make merely material gains. But the material gains should be the result *of* well chosen spiritual purposes and intents, and thus may it be said of thee, as in the days of yore, that the very stars fought for thee.

Reading 1726–1

First, in *material* conditions, we will find those of a secular life that has to do with wheels, or machinery, or things of motive force, will be of the greatest interest and of those elements *through* which—or in the sale, or representative, or agent, or such—may the entity gain of material conditions; but first must entity find *self* and set an ideal for self in *spiritual* matters, in *mental* attributes, in *mental* attainments; for remembering that Mind is the Builder, and that the spirit forces is that which is the active force from which, of which, man may use same for material gains or material detriments; for the *spirit* is willing, the *flesh* is often weak, and guided awry must bring for consternations—as they have in the past. Show self friendly, would self have *friends*. Seek through channels that there has been service rendered; not as an eyeservice, that one may become beholden to another; and do not pat another on the back simply to be patted; but speak gently, affectionately, one with another; with brotherly love *preferring* one another, and keep self unspotted from *tainted* things, *questionable* positions, *questionable* conditions. So act, as to look every man in the face and to be able to tell them that, that I have committed is an open book, and he who runs may read; that I have done may all do likewise. *Act* in *that* manner, and the sureness of self may be found in the material, in the mental things—for God is not a respecter of persons; neither is He short armed, either in giving that as will mete out for the keeping of the will one with another; neither is He short sighted in that as is committed in willful negligence, or willful disobedience, for he that abhorreth good loveth evil, and he that buildeth contention shall suddenly be destroyed—and that without mercy. Show mercy and loving kindness, then, would same be had.

Reading 1743–2

But know, that which is material must have first had its inception in the spiritual—and has grown according to *mental* application respecting same to constructive forces in the lives of individuals, things, conditions, or from whatever phase it may be judged.

Hence in the application of self, forget not the *sources* of *all* power as may be manifested in the earth.

Reading 1947–1

For as He gave, "If I go not away the spirit of truth cometh not." What meaneth this? Not merely the passing. For it was the moving of the spirit that brought materiality into existence as a *thing*, as a condition, for the souls and spirits and minds of men! And thus *He is* the way, as He is the mind, and without Him there is no other way.

Reading 1992–4

(Q) Regarding the publication advised in Nov. 1940, is it necessary to complete it by this fall?

(A) It should be better understood by seekers of truth regarding time and space as related to conditions in individuals' lives.

As is at times conceived by the mental attitudes of individuals, that which is to come into materialization—as a book, a manuscript, or even a service as related to others must pass through its *natural* laws; or there *are* laws governing same that are ever uniform.

An idea, an *ideal*, first has its spiritual inception, then its mental conceiving, and then the physical reactions that make or bring same into materialization.

As to the time of this publication, then—there must be at least the mental concept fully analyzed, completed; for the spiritual concept is a part of the entity.

Then, it may be a little later; but don't delay too long.

Reading 1998–1

But know, all has its concept in spirit—then mind; and mind is the builder.

Reading 1999–1

For remember, *mind* is the builder between the things spiritual (from which all emanate) and that which is material (which is the manifestation that mind seeks to bring ever into the experience of all).

Reading 2062–1

Hence again the injunction—look upon all phases; for there is the mental, the material and the spiritual, and these are the phases of man's reaction and man's activity. Do not apply the law of the spiritual in material things, nor the material in spiritual things. Remember that mind is the builder, and the spirit giveth life. And as ye use and dwell upon such, be sure thy ideal is in Him.

Reading 2247–1

But keep the spiritual life first. The mental and material should be the outgrowth, the result of spiritual attainments.

Reading 2281–1

Depart not from the faith thou findest in Him, and may it be renewed as the spirit ever is within thee. For the spirit is the life. The life is the purpose, the desire. Make them sure in Him.

Reading 2322–2

Know that all must first be conceived from the spiritual, and then magnified or grown through the mental application as an experience coming into material application in the lives of others.

(Q) Can suggestions be made as to how self mastery can be developed; that is, will power and initiative?

(A) Study that from the spiritual angle, if there would be that power, that might to succeed. For, as has been given, all first finds concept in the spiritual. The mental is the builder. This is true in planning the life, the relationships, and every phase of man's existence or experience.

Reading 2328–1

First, know thine own ideals—physical, mental, spiritual. Know that the spiritual and mental, and the material, must arise from that which is of spiritual concept; for only the spirit *and* mental are eternal, and only that of the mental that is spiritual in its concept—or creative in its relationships to things, conditions, experiences, places or individuals.

Reading 2357–1

Yes, we have the body and those conditions as surround same, [2357]. Now, we find there are those conditions as are abnormal for this body, and these may, in the correct application of those conditions and elements necessary, be brought to a much better and a nearer normal functioning of this body. While conditions are aggravated at times, and while seemingly there is little that may be accomplished in the physical to correct some of the conditions that disturb the body, there should first be gained the consciousness by this body that there are those elements in the physical condition of each body that will bring that for the physical functioning of that body that necessary conditions for the body to meet the needs of the body, in the physical, then mental, the moral, and the spiritual welfare of the conditions. Spirit is life, whether related to the physical functioning of the atomic forces within the system or whether that of the mental being of a body, and these must coordinate in the proper direction one with another, just as much as it is necessary for a physical functioning organ to coordinate with the rest of the system. For instance, here, with this body, there have been times when seemingly little or nothing would be assimilated or digested by the body. The necessity of assimilation is as much necessary as the desire for food; for what profit it a body to desire to eat, will the food eaten not assimilate and build that necessary for the sustenance and replenishing of the physical body? There is seen in the physical forces that there has existed, and does exist, certain disturbances in the nervous system. These have to do with both the cerebro-spinal and sympathetic nerve system. In the physical functioning of a body, the subligations or impingements of nerve or nerve plexuses, or nerve branches, become a *physical* action, and these in their turn produced, or produce, physical results; while conditions or disturbances in plexus that control, or are controlled by certain reflexes from the cerebro-spinal to the sympathetic system, may not so easily be directed by the removal of pressure in a portion of the body. What is active upon such conditions, then, that these may be aided? That of the *physical* is the vibratory rate at which the nerve functions to produce coordination in the functioning of the system, as related to the *sensory* organism or as is seen with this body, there are disturbances in the functioning of *organs* of the sensory system. These organs possess, and have, their individual machine apparatus for the functioning of the system in the direction in which that organism or organ is to function, or its own modus operandi is within itself a portion of the whole, yet dependent upon the coordination of both the cerebro-spinal and sympathetic to function in its proper relation with that organ of the system, that that as is assimilated, that as is builded in the system, may produce that *necessary* for the proper vibratory forces as to bring the result of the condition desired, or, as in this case, in the hearing, or as in the feeling. The auditory forces, then, abnormal to the conditions as should be created in this body here, [2357] we are speaking of.

Reading 2390-1

Numbers, too, become at times an influence; as three and its multiples being the phases of the entity in its various moods, or in its various manners of seeking. For, the entity finds—within itself—there is the physical, with all its emotions; the mental with its abilities to grasp and to build and to *change* the aspects of the physical if they be purely of the bodily forces or those conditions or thoughts or individual experiences; as well as the spiritual from which emanates the essence of all power, might and strength! Rely upon that more.

Reading 2408-1

In material manifestation, or the activities of these principles in a causation or three-dimensional world, one gradually realizes then the less of self and the more of world, one gradually realizes then the less of self and the more of the creative forces in the experience; thus bringing one closer to the understanding that like begets like—that what is sown in spirit may *grow* in mind, may find fruit in materiality—and that this changed may be just the reverse—that the dwelling upon material influence of selfish natures separates spirit from the control of mind, the builder.

Reading 2533–6

That is as the spirit. And as the spirit builds, as the spirit forms in its activity in mind, the mind becomes then the builder. The mind is not the spirit, it is a companion to the spirit; it builds a pattern. And this is the beginning of how self may raise that expectancy of its period of activity in the earth. And this is the beginning of thy ideal. Of what? Of that the soul should, does, will, can, must, accomplish in this experience!

Reading 2647–1

This is lack of self-confidence. This is lack of the *ideal* that is spiritual. For, know, all things material have first their inception in the spiritual. Then they give or take form in the mental, finding expression in the material. Illustrate this in that as brings to mind the concept of the music of nature, the music of the spheres, the music of the birds, the poetic expressions that oft rise to thy mind. These gradually give impressions.

Reading 2709–1

One of noble purposes, and given to good works towards others, especially that as relates to building of the mental abilities of an individual. In this respect there may be given that to the entity here, which—correlated with those ideas as have been and are being building within self towards self's development—would be well to apply in this present experience; that is, the life of every atomic force is the *spirit* of same. The mental is the builder, and the physical or sensuous manifestation is the result—and that life projects itself in that manner in which it is directed by that builded in the continuity of the life force as is radiated through that builded. See?

Reading 2727–1

First, as to thy ideal of moral and mental relationships—know that these are altogether founded in spiritual aspects. For, as the body finds itself—it is body, mind, soul. The soul lives on, builded by the mind. The body is the material manifestation. Know thy ideal.

Reading 2747–1

First, find self—and know thy own ideal, spiritually, mentally, materially. And know that the material fadeth away, the mental may bring life or death according to the choice of the mind itself.

Then in mind and in body the entity must have its life in spirit. For, this alone abideth forever.

Reading 2751–1

(Q) *How may I help my daughter, [. . .], to solve her marital problem?*

(A) These can best be studied in the light of those suggestions indicated as to the application of self through the various experiences in the earth.

Remember, if the spiritual is put first and foremost, if the purpose of an individual is in the *right* direction, the *material* happenings will eventually come right. These may at times appear confusing and as being contradictory, but the law of the Lord is *perfect*.

To enable an individual to find these is the understanding where *all* marital relationships may be best understood.

Individuals do not meet by chance. They *are* necessary in the experiences of others, though they may not always use their opportunities in a spiritual way or manner.

Thus the injunction—study to show thyself approved unto thy ideal, which *is* thy God. If ye make thyself god, if ye make thy hopes, thy wants, thy purposes thy god, they become selfish, they become monsters, they become destroying influences.

Teach, give instruction, even as ye did in the Egyptian experience. There ye aided. Now ye may aid; not by material.

And *do not* condemn anyone!

Reading 2772-1

For, life is God, or eternity, and thus is a continuous thing. Various consciousnesses in various spheres of activity are only as a part of the experience, as the mind is the controlling and the building force in the physical being. For, mind is the builder. That which is of the spirit is that which is proposed, while that in the physical is as the result of material application.

Reading 2776-1

Find thy ideal, spiritually, mentally and materially. Know that all force has its expression first in spirit. True, mind is the control—through that activity comes the material expression of same.

Reading 2786-1

These may become stumblingblocks in the entity's experience even in the present. Look to that which is an ideal, and be sure it is founded in that of spiritual import. For, every fact has its inception in spirit; mind is the builder, the material expression is the outcome of one of these upon the other. The spirit is of creation, or God; the mind is as of an individual taking hold upon both materiality and spirituality. The choice is in the hands of the individual. Use thy talents well.

Reading 2787-1

We find in Jupiter the universal consciousness. Notice its position, though, in thy awareness. Move it toward the front, rather than toward the end. For, first in spirit, then in mind, then is the materialization. For, mind is the builder; even as ye find thy body, thy mind, thy soul the three-dimensional experience of an individual that become comparable with the Father, the Son and the Holy Spirit. The Son is the Mind. He *is* the way. So the mind of self is the way.

Reading 2788-1

The entity seeks to know first causes. Remember, these arise from spiritual concepts. For, it is first in spirit, then in mind, then the material manifestation; whether this is association with individuals or things, or whether it has to do with universal activity as in the nature of things. For, it is the purpose with which individual man makes application to the things about him, that brings about the physical or material result. "With what spirit, with what purpose, do ye these things?"

Reading 2801–1

Now, in the physical, mental and spiritual forces in this body, which complete the entity at this time, we have a good manifestation of the entity in a psychological understanding and manifestation of the psychology of an entity, for we find the mental rules in this entity, as it should in the earth plane, and the physical is under subjugation of the mental proclivities of the entity. That is, we have in this entity one well rounded to a completion of the forces in the earth plane, for there is much spiritual understanding with the mental forces, and the entity needs only to keep all the forces well rounded in that straight and narrow way that leads to the perfect understanding.

As to the physical conditions, we find in the present forces these are very good in many respects. There are some conditions that the body needs from the physical, from the mental, from the spiritual aspect, to be wary of, for the soul, spirit and the physical must ever remember the physical body, the material body, is but the temple through which the mental forces, with the will, builds to that I AM that must ever live, and without the perfect balanced forces the best cannot be given or manifested through the present entity's forces.

Reading 2813–1

First, know thy ideals—physical, mental and spiritual. And know the physical result is first conceived in spirit, acted upon by mind, and then manifested in the material—with what spirit ye entertain.

Reading 2900–2

Know thy ideal spiritually, the application of same mentally, and ye will find the material things will come in their own way and time.

Reading 2938-1

For, in the material world the spiritual concept is the basis of the trend, or of the mind; and from same arises the material results. When such relationship, or when any relationship is altered otherwise, it may become a stumblingstone rather than a steppingstone for unfoldment.

Reading 2995-3

Know, then, that these also apply to the entity concerning same: The body, mind and soul of the entity are one. They are represented here as a physical body—very good in many respects. A very analytical mind, but as indicated, one who tends to draw judgments rather severely. Know that there are laws pertaining to such in mind as well as in spiritual and in material. For whatever there may be is first conceived in spirit. It is acted upon by mind. Dependent, then, upon what the mind of the entity holds as its ideal, or as to what form or manner it would give . . . by and through what spirit it would build in its mental self.

Reading 3053-3

Many stress spirituality when the mind is used as the measuring stick. Many stress physical manifestation when mind is used as the measuring stick. Many interpret spiritual things and attempt to use physical activity as the measuring stick. Many attempt to interpret spiritual things, using the mind as the measuring stick. But each phase of thine own experience should be interpreted in its proper sphere of activity, so that when ye interpret thy music, thy love, thy friendships, thy associations, thy activities with others, it will be in the proper sphere according to thy whole purpose in the earth—to glorify thy Maker; if there would be the full interpretation of "The Lord thy God is one" and "Thou shalt love thy brother as thyself." O that men would find, there is nothing mentioned here about the physical or the mind, but the spiritual attitude one takes in self respecting such!

Reading 3064-1

When the Appliance is used, do use the period for meditation upon *spiritual* things; knowing that all healing, all correcting of the spiritual and of the mental life must come from the divine within, and the results in the physical being will be in keeping with that which is developed in the spiritual self.

Reading 3083-1

Yet, learn the lesson: that physical must be met in the physical, that mental must be met in the mental, and that spiritual is the directing force—but mind is the builder.

Reading 3132-1

The material is of the earth-earthy. The spiritual is of the heavenly or the motivative forces. The mental is ever the builder.

That as would be manifested must first be in spirit, then in mind, then in material activity. For, this is the evolution of the earth, the evolution of things, the evolution of ideas and of ideals. For, He came into the earth that through Him man might have access again to the grace and mercy of those spiritual forces that are the directing ideals of each soul-entity.

Reading 3184-1

Then, these are the things the entity should analyze the more in self—as will be seen from the periods of expression in the earth—as to what are the promptings of the individual's urges. For each individual finds the motivative influence of its life within its own self, and that is correct—as was stated of old by the lawgiver; Think not as to who will descend from heaven to give a message or who would come from over the sea that ye might learn and understand. For lo it is within thine own heart, thine own mind. Thy body is indeed the temple of the living God. He has promised to meet thee and, know that all in the mental, all in the material, has its inception, it conception, in spirit, in purpose, in hope, in desire. Know thy relationship, then, first, with that ye hope for. For life (or God), immortality of the soul, is real; as may be seen from thine own urges—if ye analyze them correctly.

Reading 3190-2

(Q) *In what way can the body control the physical through the mental?*
(A) The mental ever controls the physical, when guided in those chan-

nels that gives the awakening in the physical of the Divine in self. In that channel may the body guide the physical through the mental, for ever will we find that the "spirit beareth witness with My Spirit," as to the control to make the mental, the physical, the spiritual in the body One with *that force* giving the life in the body.

Reading 3198-3

What is manifested in the material affairs or activities of the entity is first perceived or conceived in the spiritual imports of the entity. These are cultivated or entertained in the mental and thus physical results are evidenced.

Reading 3241-1

(Q) *What spiritual qualities should be stressed?*

(A) Know that all that is in material manifestation is first of spirit; then by mind (the builder) is brought into realization. Then by the power of the might that is in Him and in His promise, keep that faith which has been indicated for the entity.

Reading 3308-1

Thus in the dedicating of thy mind, of thy body, may the soul express—through the activities of mind and body—that which is in keeping with that the Master gave—"If ye love Me, keep My commandments, and I—and the Father—will come and abide with thee." These are not merely symbols, signs or tenets, but may be made practical in the lives of individuals that ye may instruct day by day; not by any set form. For, if the Lord is one, He is in the storm as in the stillness, in the stars as in the sand in *activity*. For life itself is the manifestation of the oneness of the Father manifested in the Son, who came to give life and it—life more abundantly. For, He is the life, the resurrection, the way. These ye should teach, these ye should practice in thy conversation, in thy daily dealings with thy fellow man.

Reading 3333-1

(Q) *How can I know I am in the right work and be contented with it?*

(A) "My spirit beareth witness with thy spirit." Not only is this applicable in spirit but in mind and in body. For, know, the Lord is one. All that becomes active in the mind is first in spirit. Then in mind does it grow. Then it materiality does it take shape.

Reading 3350-1

Thus innately the entity is ever desiring to try something new. This is well, provided the basis of such is builded upon truth. For truth in any clime is ever the same—it is law. And love is law, law is love. Love is God, God is Love. It is the universal consciousness, the desire for harmonious expressions for the good of all, that is the heritage in man, if there is the acceptance of the way and manner such may be applied, first in the spiritual purpose and then in the mental application, and the material success will be pleasing to any.

Reading 3351-1

Know that of such, yea of people, would be known that faults and successes do not come from thought. Thought is the builder, but spirit is the motivating force. What spirit do you entertain? If it be of God, it can not fail, if it be of self or the devil a failure may be in the offing, dependent upon the measure with which ye mete same—as through the experience of the entity as Marcelle Ney.

Reading 3359-1

Find that, and ye will begin then with the correct attitude. For, that we find in spirit taketh form in mind. Mind becomes the builder. The physical body is the result.

Reading 3376-2

But what is thy yardstick of ideals? All that is material once existed in spirit, or the soul of the entity. Mind becomes the builder, the physical becomes the result. It depends, then, upon the materials—or the spirit with which one is prompted.

Reading 3394-2

In Jupiter an ennobling influence has made the entity ever mindful of the need of a universal consciousness towards the follow man, even for material gains in the earth. There needs to be a warning that there be the more application for the spiritual needs, the spirit of the law of love and of friendship, rather than the letter of the law. For those who would have friends or who would succeed materially must begin with the spirit that is entertained. If the spirit is for self or is of a selfish nature, or one of spite or greed, it must eventually turn upon thee.

Reading 3424–1

Also in Jupiter we find the interest in morality, religion, good living, personality. These shall all be approached, to be sure, from individuality; and the basis of the individuality of an entity must come from its ideal spiritually. For all is born first in spirit, then in mind, then it may become manifested in the material plane. For God moved and the heavens and the earth came into being. God is spirit. Man with his soul, that may be a companion to the Creative Forces, is of that same source. Thus to grow in grace and knowledge, one applies, one has, one uses one's spiritual self. And with what spirit we apply, we grow also in mind and in body.

Reading 3463–1

Astrologically we find urges from Mercury, Saturn, Mars, Uranus. These bring the high mental abilities. In Saturn there is ofttimes not the consideration of others nor the sources from which all good must arise. For it can only come from one source, and it is not material alone. The material is merely the result. It must be builded in spiritual purposes. It must be builded according to the spirit with which a soul–entity is entertained or moved.

Reading 3481–1

Individuals can become too zealous or too active without consideration of the physical, mental and spiritual. True, all influences are first spiritual; but the mind is the builder and the body is the result. Spiritualizing the body without the mind being wholly spiritualized may bring such results as we find indicated here, so as to raise even the kundaline forces in the body without their giving full expression.

Reading 3513-1

For that which occurs in physical or in mind is first prompted in spirit, and thus are the activities of the entity correlated one to another, not only in this experience but throughout the consciousness of the entity in the various spheres or varied periods of material activity with a physical consciousness.

Reading 3541-1

But first we would give these: Know that all that comes into materialization or into physical being is first patterned in mind and in spirit. Mind is the builder, and your purpose is dependent upon what spirit—or what mortar, what water—those things that go to make materiality active in the earth—you use, as to what is the character of the body mind or structure that ye, as an entity, create.

Reading 3582-2

For as the entity realizes, there is little or nothing that happens by chance, but ever after a pattern, a law. And that the entity may build in the mind from the spiritual, that it accepts as its director alters results that may be had in the experience of the individual—in the same measure as was asked "Master, who sinned—this man or his parents, that he was born blind?"

Reading 3590-2

The spiritual self is life, the activity of the mental and of the physical is of the soul—and thus a soul-body.

Reading 3611-1

The entity must learn that this must be as much in the mental, or more. For the physical is the result of the spiritual ideals, and the mind as the builder brings those results. True, the body must at times have its discipline, but this is rather of mind and spirit as well as physical discipline.

Reading 3639-1

Then, the entity should become well founded in relationship with

Creative Forces. For any activity begins first in spirit, then in mind, and then in the material world. And mind is the builder. It is that which builds for whatever may be the contributing factor from the abilities of individuals, as well as self's application in same.

Reading 3704–1

(Q) *What is the purpose of this life on earth for me?*

(A) As indicated, in applying self in greater welfare activities for others, and in the preparation of and in building the home. First it must be spiritual, then it must be mental and then it may be in the physical.

Reading 3902–2

As urges latent and manifested, many are the manifestations in the consciousness and in the urges of the entity indicating unusual abilities to manifest in a material world. From the urges, from sojourns during the interims we find Mercury, Mars, Venus, Jupiter. No better array might be set, and yet—as in spirit, so in mind—these must be attuned, used, applied. For though there may be purpose, ability, strength, without being used it is nil and of none effect.

Reading 3975–1

Yes, we have the body here. We find there are abnormal conditions in this body, [3975] we are speaking of. These have more to do with specific causes in the physical. Keep in touch with this here if you would get this. The conditions as we have given here have more to do in the physical body than we have to do with that between the spirit and soul or mental force in the body here for there are in the physical body the material change or difference that must be brought about to make the whole body work in accord and create a perfect equilibrium throughout the whole system in this body. If we would correct the condition so that the whole life giving force or fluids in the body have their course in their proper accord throughout the system and could give to all the portions of this body the life giving forces then we will find that the rejuvenation of all forces of the body will be brought to normal and that we have the physical forces with the mental and divine forces all carried out throughout their whole forces in the body and bring the mental and spirit forces to a development to better understanding of itself. The physical force in this system has been brought into this body that it may learn and develop more through the mental and spiritual forces that it is to carry on with these from time to time. This it must understand in self.

Reading 4035-1

We find in Mars the very decided points or ideas or stands that the entity may take on subjects; but as warned concerning the experience before this as a critic, if you criticize then you may expect to be criticized yourself. For the law of the Lord is perfect and it is as applicable in man as in the universe, as in nature, as in the realms of spirit itself. For the first principle is that the Lord, the God of the universe is one. What is effective or active in spirit (where it forms first) must be active and must influence the imaginative influences of an individual entity. For the entity finds itself a body, a mind, a soul—three; or the earth consciousness as a three-dimensional plane in one.

Reading 4041-1

Know these as facts: That which is manifested physically or mentally has its concept or urge arising from the spiritual aspects of the entity, or the spirit, the purpose, the sources, the urges entertained by the entity. If such purposes and ideals or urges are of and through creative forces, then the mental (as the builder) may become constructive or creative. Then the physical or final manifestation will be good. That the changes may come doesn't necessarily indicate that the spiritual urge is in error but that the manner or way of application in the mental may be in the wrong direction.

Reading 4143-1

In the mental we find those abilities to mete out much that may be helpful to others in their understanding their relationships with their fellow man, as well as their relationship with the spiritual influences that may be manifest in the material plane. Materially, we find spiritual forces are the life, the background, the basis for all activity; the mental is the builder; the physical is the result that accrues from such activity in the material or in the carnal plane.

Reading 4405-1

In the physical forces, keep fit—keep the *mental* attuned properly, and the *spiritual* life *will* guide in all things! Oft is it considered by individuals that the spiritual life and mental life are things apart. They *must* be one—they *are* one, even though individuals attempt to separate. The *spirit* is the life, the motive force, that behind all life itself, and the mind-physical and the mind of the soul—or that spirit force itself—is guiding, directing—not always guarding, but may be trained in that direction. Hence, seek that of the spiritual within self *first*, and *all these* things of *earthly* nature will be *added* in their proper place, their proper association, their proper connections. Ready for questions.

Reading 4609-1

In the urge in conditions existent in the present physical relations with the universal forces, we may find much with this entity worthy of study by those who hold to tenets respecting continuity of life and its relation with the varied appearances of an entity through the experiences in the earth's plane; for to the physiognomist there is presented that, in the mental and physical being of the entity or body present, which would be proof positive of that law given as concerning how that life manifested in the earth plane is first the life spiritual, the life mental, the physical a result of that builded and coming in manifested form irrespective of that that has been often misapplied or misdirected towards environmental or hereditary conditions; for we find the lives of those whom this entity's being in the present plane manifested through were in accord with that same law, and brought into being that which—through the existent conditions of environmental nature—presented the channel for that manifested life as builded by the individual entity, and the entity sought that channel for its manifestation in the earth's plane at that stage of its development, or—as man would physically call it—at that time.

Reading 4722-1

(Q) *Any spiritual advice for the body?*

(A) Awaken that within self to the abilities, to the qualities that the body may experience through the activity of the spiritual forces within self, that will give the reactions and make the effects as may be created in the physical; for the spiritual is the life, the mental is the builder, and the physical or material is the result.

Reading 4866–2

As has been outlined, this also must be taken into consideration, as the body seeks for those developments in self from the mental and material conditions in the affairs of self—that as self sets as its ideal. What it would work toward must have a great deal to do with what may be called an entirely successful operation, an entirely successful development for the body; for what the body sets as its ideal, whether that which is wholly of the material or that which is a well balanced spiritual, mental and material condition, will be those developments; for the activity—whether of wholly material conditions, mental conditions, or of spiritual conditions—is the *spirit* with which an entity, a body, goes about its activity. If the life is to become wholly mechanical, or wholly material minded, then only the material will be the natural result, and this will *not* bring contentment—nor will it satisfy. If the ideal will be set as a well balanced self, knowing that the spirit, the life—that is, the spirit *is* the life, the mental attitude is the development or the builder, then the results will be in that comparison as to the activity that is given in respect to these attitudes.

Reading 5001–1

These are problems you are meeting in self in the present. For ye had the same companion through that experience. Thus let that of duty from the spiritual self be the guiding influence. For the entity finds self with a body which it can get along with very well! It can use its own judgments, its own appetites, its own activities. The mind becomes something else! and these influences should be governed by spiritual import, spiritual purpose. Know that what is first conceived is in spirit. In mind does it grow to an activity which becomes either creative or self-satisfying, self-gratifying.

Reading 5118–1

Before this the entity was in the land of the present sojourn. Hence those attractions that have brought the entity to the present environs. For the entity is a "sensitive", as indicated in the manner in which it studies the anatomical structure, as well as the mind structure. Not enough stress is put on the spiritual, for the sources. For, what comes in mind, in materiality, must first have been created in the spirit. For the earth was first without form and void. So is mind, or matter. It is first a desire, a consciousness, a fluid, a gas. It is united, it becomes, as it were, as a "feeling" for. So may the entity in itself find the same. These are of particular interest to the entity.

Reading 5502–3

(Q) *What can [257] further do in his daily life to show himself more approved unto the Giver of these gifts?*

(A) Study to show thyself approved unto God, avoiding the appearances of evil, knowing that as the acts of thine going-ins and coming-outs [are] that reflection of the God ye would serve. If that God be money, power, position, fame, these must reflect in the lives and the life of the acts of self. Will those forces as were made manifest as of old when Abraham [was] called to go out to make a peculiar people, a different nation, so again may the body hear that called as when offering in the temple that "Mine people have wandered astray", yet in the little here, the word there, the precept and example, may they again know Jehovah in His Holy Place.

Necessary that each individual have their own problems given that attention as seemeth to them necessary, but as and when ones [are] well-grounded in the truths of the universe that may know through that given them that the spirit is life, the spirit of service is strength, and [that it] aids in every condition in man's experience.

Reading 5534–1

(Q) *What will his attitude be when he returns?*

(A) In answer to that as is desired in self; for desire is of a threefold nature, and that builded in self finds its response in another, and as there is the *sincere* desire to build in the mental being of any in which such relationships have existed, as in this condition, that will be builded—for life, in all its phases, is of the threefold nature. *Spirit* is willing; *mind* is the builder; the *result* is that *manifested* in the material conditions as surround a body. That attitude, then, will be that as has been builded, as has been desired in self as related to another.

Reading 5642-3

We have the body here—we have had this before, you see. Now we find there are improvements in the physical forces of this body since last we had same here. There are many conditions to be considered respecting those conditions that exist in the physical being of the body, and while there arise from time to time those elements that are of a disturbing and discouraging nature to the body, these [the epilepsy attacks] will of necessity have to be by the body put in the background and not allow these conditions—because they do occur occasionally—to gain control over the mental body; for while physical conditions are reacting to the mental being, the mental body *is* the builder. The physical is the result, and the spiritual will build that as is builded in the mental being, and a physical result is then amenable to outside influences that are mental, material, and physical. Hence there are being applied in the physical being of this body those conditions that, while these are material—and while the mental body is in the condition of being disturbed, this gives rise to those conditions of discouragement. This must have the outside influence to give the proper incentive in a correlated effect or correlated manner to this body, so that the whole physical reaction will be in keeping with that as the mental being would have the body be. Then, be consistent—persistent—in the spiritual, mental and physical application of all those conditions that apply to the physical body, to the material body, to the mental body, and the *spiritual* will guide and lead aright. For we are one in Him, and ourselves may only get in the way of a full development. Then keep those, as yet, as have been given, and be patient in well-doing. Do not be overcome, but overcome evil with good. Materially, mentally, physically, apply this in the body. Do that.

Reading 5642–4

Keep the inhalant; also keep the manipulations as often as is *convenient* for the body to do so. Keep in the open. Do not overtax the mind, but keep sufficient physical exercise to keep proper coordination, and we will find the near normal conditions will yet come to this body. Keep the mental in attunement to the spiritual side of life, and remember that the spiritual will build that, that the *mental* will attune itself for a physical or materialization in the flesh; for the spiritual forces are the same one day after another, and unto the end.

Reading 5680–1

In the spiritual development of self: These are as the greater forces that come to everyone, for, as is seen, while the body physical presents as a unit a oneness, yet same is made up of the spiritual, the mental and the physical. The spiritual the creator, the mental the builder, the material—that of the result of a life, a thought, a deed; for thoughts are deeds and may be miracles or crimes in their execution and the end thereof.

Reading 5735–1

That, Life is in that way of continuity; and Life is *all*; and no one portion of Life is the whole; for Life is that given of the *spirit*; and the Soul is as the individual. The mental—whether that of a sensuous consciousness or of the super, or the objective consciousness—is the Builder; and that *builded*, whether in the physical or soul body, is the Result.

3

●

Soul

Reading 281–41

Ye all find yourselves confused at times respecting from whence ye came and whither ye goeth. Ye find yourselves with bodies, with minds—not all beautiful, not all clean, not all pure in thine own sight or in thy neighbor's. And there are many who care more for the outward appearance than that which prompts the heart in its activity or in its seeking . . .

Many say that ye have no consciousness of having a soul—yet the very fact that ye hope, that ye have a desire for better things, the very fact that ye are able to be sorry or glad, indicates an activity of the mind that takes hold upon something that is not temporal in its nature—something that passeth not away with the last breath that is drawn but that takes hold upon the very sources of its beginning—the *soul*—that which was made in the image of thy Maker—not thy body, no—not thy mind, but thy *soul* was in the image of thy Creator.

Reading 361–9

Then so live that you may ever look *every* man in the face and see the reflection of your God. For the soul of every man is the image of thy Maker.

Reading 262–89

As to commenting upon the subject Destiny of the Soul: As man finds himself in the consciousness of a material world, materiality has often, in the material-minded, blotted out the consciousness of a soul.

Man in his former state, or natural state, or permanent consciousness, *is* soul. Hence in the beginning all were souls of that creation, with the body as of the Creator—of the spirit forces that make manifest in using same in the various phases or experiences of consciousness for the activity.

Reading 416–2

When there is the thought or the activity of the body in any particular environ, this every activity makes for the impressions upon the soul. For, the soul is that body which lives on into infinity, and is the companion of the particular body only in a particular or individual experience.

Reading 1587–1

For *only* in man is there the existence of the soul that is not just universal, but individual; capable of becoming as a god, as one with the Creative Forces.

Reading 815–7

(Q) *Since the soul of each individual is part of the One Soul, the Great Soul, or what Emerson calls "the Oversoul"—why then is it that its impulsions in each of us are not clearly and singularly heard? And what is meant by the phrase: "a soul lesson"—as if the soul instead of being our guide and destiny, needed any lessons from the self, the incarnating entity?*

(A) This, to perfectly understand, might require the whole period here of interpreting. But the entity forgets that God, the Creative Force, in creating souls—with the attributes of the "oversoul," or the One—endowed each soul with *free will*, in its movement through time and space—being endowed then with a consciousness in whatever dimension of manifestation the soul moves in that period of expression.

God, the First Cause, has not willed that any soul should perish, and has with every temptation given a way, a means of escape.

The entity or soul, in any given period in time of manifestation in space, may use those attributes of that phase of its consciousness in whatever realm it moves, according to the dictates of that which impels it—through its will.

If the soul were at all periods, all manifestations, to keep in that perfect accord, or law, with the "oversoul," or the First Cause, or the Soul from which it comes, then there would be only a continuous at-onement with the First Cause.

But when an entity, a soul, uses a period of manifestation—in whatever realm of consciousness—to its *own indulgences*, then there is need for the lesson, or for the soul understanding or interpreting, or to become aware of he error of its way.

What, then, was the first cause of this awareness?

It was the eating, the partaking, of knowledge; knowledge without wisdom—or that as might bring pleasure, satisfaction, gratifying—not of the soul but of the phases of expression in that realm in which the manifestation was given. Thus in the three–dimensional phases of con-sciousness such manifestations become as pleasing to the eye, pleasant to the body appetites. Thus the interpretation of the experience, or of that first awareness of deviation from the divine law, is given in the form as of eating of the tree of knowledge.

Who, what influence, caused this—ye ask?

It was that influence which had, or would, set itself in opposition to the souls remaining, or the entity remaining, in that state of at–onement.

What, then, is the first cause of man's expression? That he may know himself to be himself and yet one with the Father; separate, yet as Fa-ther, Son and Holy Spirit are one, so the body, the mind, the soul of an entity may also be at–one with the First Cause.

Reading 900–17

(Q) It has been given that the soul is the spiritual force that animates or gives life to the body. What is spirit? What is spiritual force? Is it corporeal or incorporeal? Where may we find the soul force in the body—in the brain, nerve centers or where?

(A) There is a vast deal of difference between spiritual and soul forces, for, as given, about each force there has been set guards or bounds. Spirit forces are the animation of *all life*-giving, life–producing forces in animate or inanimate forces. Spiritual elements become corporeal when we speak of the spiritual body in a spiritual entity; then composed of spirit, soul and the superconsciousness.

In the soul's forces, and its dwelling in man, we find the animation, the spiritual element, the soul that developing element, and contained in the brain, in the nerve, in the centers of the whole system. As to the specific centers, nearer those centers of the sensory system, physically speaking.

In the conditions, then, we find when soul and spirit take flight from the animate forces of a human, we find the deadening of all the centers of the sensory system, with the vitality of the solar plexus system, with the gland of the medulla oblongata, these then controlling the forces, and life becomes extinct, with soul and spirit, with the superconscious forces, gone. Then, we have as this:

Spiritual element, the vitality, produces the motive forces of the entity, whether physical or spiritual. Spiritual forces being the life, the reproductive principle; the soul, the development principle. As we have manifested, or illustrated, in the physical body in nerve tissue: There becomes that principle of the nerve action and the nerve in action. That is, with the expression of some condition bringing distress in the body, the active principle is the spirit. The nerve is the soul, for development.

Reading 1096–4

Not that this may become burdensome, but that there may be for the entity a more perfect understanding:

Each soul is a portion of the Divine. Motivating that soul–body is the spirit of divinity. The soul is a companion of, a motivative influence in, the activities of an entity throughout its experiences in whatever sphere of consciousness it may attain perception.

Hence each soul is a universe in itself.

This entity came into an experience during those early activities of Ahasuerus, or Xerxes as called by the Grecians, that there might be during those experiences a fulfilling of the promises that had been made to a peculiar people.

Hence each soul finds itself ever in the hands of a *living* Intelligence, a living God.

Not that it, the entity, hasn't its own free will, but it—the entity or soul—develops either to a oneness with that Universal Consciousness or in opposition to same.

At times there may be a paralleling of purposes. There may be experiences that this entity or that entity may be at a tangent to the Universal Consciousness.

In that experience, though belittled by those that were in a development of a *personal* ego, those activities of the entity *filled* a parallel with that universality of love in holding to that which made for the elevating of the activities of others to that which cries aloud in its seeking for expression—that all souls, men *and* women, stand as *one* before that Universal Consciousness, that Throne of grace, of mercy, that has brought the souls of men into materiality in body, that there might be an awareness more and more of *their* relationship—yea, their kinship to that *source* of right, justice, mercy, patience, long-suffering, love.

Hence the entity in that particular experience found itself in that position of championing the cause of those that had through the timidity of the activities from the expressions been kept in that way of woman being the weaker vessel. Yet in the very activity there came to the forefront that expression which found its *crowning* when the virgin gave birth to Him who became the Savior of men!

In those surroundings of egotism, then, in those surroundings of faults and faultfindings, the entity *gave* to those peoples, to the world, a concrete example of the *freeing* of the souls of those that, though in body they be joined to those in power or authority, seek—their individualities, their souls, their entities seek and make expressions in a material world!

Then, in making application of same in the present, naturally there arise those questionings within self, as to how, why should *this* entity at *this* time again manifest and seek expression, when there is being given to the activities of the earth the thoughts of the sons of men, the thoughts and the delving into the abilities of the daughters of men? That it *again* may give expression to the *freedom* of the soul even under the laws that have been made by man, for these' be not the laws of the Universal Love.

Reading 2834–1

Know, first, that each soul is a manifestation of an influence in the earth that we may call a son of God. Thus there are the needs that each soul recognize the relationship it bears with that force or power in the earth, and behave in such a manner as to be worthy of that grace given by the Creative Force.

Reading 2879–1

Man finds himself a body, a mind, a soul. The body is self–evident. The mind also is at times understood. The soul or the spiritual portion is hoped for, and one may only discern same from a spiritual consciousness.

Reading 3062–2

For, the soul is equal with the universal consciousness or purpose, or God consciousness—as it may be termed, and thus is a part of all it has experienced; having an influence upon, and being influenced by all of these, according to the will of the entity.

Reading 3559–1

There is body, there is mind, there is soul. They each have their attributes, they each have their limitations. The soul, in a material world, is controlled by mind and body.

Reading 3744–2
[Background: From a series on psychic phenomena]

(Q) What is the soul of a body?

(A) That which the Maker gave to every entity or individual in the beginning, and which is seeking the home or place of the Maker.

Reading 3744–4
[Background: From a series on psychic phenomena]

The study from the human standpoint, of subconscious, subliminal, psychic, soul forces, is and should be the great study for the human family, for through self man will understand its Maker when it understands its relation to its Maker, and it will only understand that through itself, and that understanding is the knowledge as is given here in this state.

Reading 487–17

What then, the entity asks, *is* a soul? What does it look like? What is its plane of experience or activity? How may ye find one? It may not be separated in a material world from its own place of abode in the body-physical, yet the soul looks through the eyes of the body—it handles with the emotions of the sense of touch—it may be aware through the factors in every sense, and thus add to its body as much as the food of the material world has made for a growing physical body in which the soul may and does indeed dwell in its passage or activity in any individual phase of an experience in the earth.

Reading 2079–1

An entity, or soul, is a spark—or a portion—of the Whole, the First Cause; and thus is a co-worker with that First Cause, or Purpose, which is the creative influence or force that is manifested in materiality.

Each entity, each soul, is endowed with self-will; that which is the force that makes it able, or gives it the capacity, to be the law, and yet complying with a universal purpose.

Reading 2283–1

Know that ye *are* a soul, and do not merely attain to one; for the spiritual activity is of the Creative Force and thus is eternal.

Reading 3003–1

As has been experienced in the mental self, there is as much reason to dwell upon the thought from whence the soul came, as it is upon whence the soul goeth. For, if the soul is eternal, it always has been—if it is always to be. And that is the basis, or the thought of Creative Force, or God. He ever was, He ever will be. And individuals, as His children, are a part of that consciousness. And it is for that purpose that He came into the earth; that we, as soul-entities, might know ourselves to be ourselves, and yet one with Him; as He, the Master, the Christ, knew Himself to be Himself and yet one with the Father.

Thus the purpose of manifestation in the material plane; that we may apply here a little, there a little, line upon line, precept upon precept, that we may become like Him.

And as the entity has through the experiences seen and aided others in the application of their efforts and their abilities to become more and more aware of their relationships to the Creative Forces or God, so may the entity—as He gave—in patience become ye aware of thy soul.

For, as indicated in the three-dimensional consciousness—the Father, the Son, the Holy Ghost—time, space and patience—man—body, mind, soul—*all* answer one to another. Hence the first law, "My spirit beareth witness with thy spirit."

These become, then, the first principles in this entity's analyzing of itself and of its activity in the earth.

As indicated in the certain periods, remember—as has been given—it is not because ye were born in May, or on the 4th of May, that such and such happened to thee. For, as a corpuscle in the body of God, ye are free-willed—and thus a co-creator with God. Thus the universe stood still, as it were, that ye might manifest in a certain period that ye had attained by thy activity in the earth. For, as He hath given in all places, *time* must be full. An individual entity's experience must be finished before the entity may either be blotted out or come into full brotherhood with the greater abilities, or the greater applications of self in the creating or finishing of that begun.

Reading 5159–2

For only the spirit and soul are eternal but they are as much a body in the eternal realms as the physical body is a body in the material realm.

Reading 5330–1

For the soul is eternal and if the entity will analyze its own self, it is body, mind and soul. Soul which longs for spiritual interpretations, mental understanding and physical harmony and rest. These are parts of the experience of every soul. One seeks rest whether young or old, and yet the physical for this body, as well as of others, needs rest, recuperation.

Reading 5749-3
[Background: From a reading for the Second Annual A.R.E. Congress]

(Q) Explain the law of the line of demarcation between soul and spirit.

(A) This is one, yet is distinct—even as the Father, the Son, the Holy Spirit is one, yet is the manifestation of a force that is capable of manifestation in the varied planes of development.

The soul is an individual, individuality, that may grow to be one with, or separate from, the whole.

The spirit is the impelling influence of infinity, or the one creative source, force, that is manifest.

Hence we find that in the physical plane we seek soul manifestation as the spirit moves same in activity.

Reading 5753-1
[Background: From a reading given at the Second Annual A.R.E. Congress regarding reincarnation]

A soul, an entity, is as real as a physical entity, and is as subject to laws as the physical body is subject to the laws in a material world and the elements thereof!

Does fire burn the soul or the physical body?

Yet, self may cast self into a fire element by doing that the soul knows to be wrong!

What would make a wrong and a right? A comparison of that the soul knows its consciousness to be in accord or contrariwise with, in relation to that which gave it existence.

Reading 5405-1
The giving of sedatives, the giving of certain classes or characters of treatment, has destroyed the ability in the physical self to respond to kindness. For, as may be found in the experience of every human soul, the soul responds to all the fruits of the spirit of truth, when even the mind and body may not. But know that mind, in the material, is the builder. Thus, with the correct—or a direct—spiritual application of the tenets of truth—patience, long-suffering, gentleness, kindness, brotherly love—there may be help.

Evolution and Destiny of the Soul

Reading 518-2

(Q) *Is it the destiny of souls that were united in the beginning to be reunited? or can they choose otherwise?*

(A) Choose otherwise.

(Q) *Were they united for a certain purpose; is that how they are drawn together?*

(A) United; for a purpose.

Reading 900-20

(Q) Is it the destiny of every spiritual entity to eventually become one with God?

(A) Unless that entity wills its banishment. As is given with man, in the giving of the soul, the will, wherewith to manifest in the entity, whether spiritual, whether material. With that, the entity, either spiritual or physical, may banish itself. Again a compliance with law; as has been given, hell was prepared for Satan and his angels, yet God has not *willed* that *any* soul should perish. Giving of will to His creation, man, that man might be one with Him, giving man the privilege of exercising his (man's) will, or exercising His (God's) will to be one with Him. As in destiny, meaning a law, compliance with a law, destined to be subject, or *being* the law. The destruction of same destined to the contribution to the destruction of such law.

Reading 826-8

(Q) *Must each soul continue to be reincarnated in the earth until it reaches perfection, or are some souls lost?*

(A) Can God lose itself, if God be God—or is it submerged, or is it as has been given, carried into the universal soul or consciousness? The *soul* is not lost; the *individuality* of the soul that separates itself is lost. The reincarnation or the opportunities are continuous until the soul has of itself become an *entity* in its whole or has submerged itself.

Reading 900-59

(Q) *Explain the different environments which the individual enters before reaching the earth plane, while in earth plane and after.*

(A) The individual entity before coming in earth's plane bears only the spirit relation to the Universal Forces with a soul to be made, through the environments of creation, equal to the created, given the free will as to how same shall be developed. Before entering the earth's plane of its own choice, or free will, developing through those spheres it chooses for its developing. In the earth's plane and spheres then becoming subject to the laws of that sphere to which it chooses its sojourn, passing through same with its urge of development taken on in the beginning, subject to the environment through which it passes for its development, and as has been given, all soul and spirit force is of the Creator, and given to the individual, which brings or makes it an individual to use as it sees fit. As illustrated in that given by Him that shows the way, the talents given to every entity those of its making, by its use, all being the same in the beginning. As the developing passes, the entity, the nearer the whole becomes one with the Creator, the nearer comes the perfect developing, for the whole law is to be one with the Creator. Yet never losing its identity, for that given in the beginning, but becoming one with the Creator as each unit of the blood itself the portion of the earthly being in its sojourn through the earth. We find in the man the every elements and representation of how the entity one with the Creator, and with the will to make same one with the Creator, with all the attributes of a creator, and with the will to make same one with Him, or rebel against that element.

Reading 2067–1

For, while there is physical evolution, there is also soul growth—not an evolution, but an awareness in material things.

Reading 2079–1

For, indeed, each entity, each soul, is in the process of evolution towards the First Cause. Much becomes evolution—much may become involution.

Reading 3357–1

We find that the astrological aspects mean little to the entity, yet they each have their place, which—as indicated—is relative. No urge exceeds the will of the individual entity, that gift from and of the Creative Forces that separates man, even the Son of man, from the rest of creation. Thus it is made to be ever as one with the Father, knowing itself to be itself and yet one with the Father, never losing its identity. For, to lose its identity is death indeed—death indeed—separation from the Creative Force. The soul may never be lost, for it returns to the One Force, but knows not itself to be itself any more.

Reading 3744–2
[Background: From a series of readings on psychic phenomena]

(Q) *Does the soul ever die?*

(A) May be banished from the Maker, not death.

(Q) *What is meant by banishment of a soul from its Maker?*

(A) Of the will as given in the beginning to choose for self as in the earthly plane, all insufficient matter is cast unto Saturn. To work out his own salvation as would be termed in the word, the entity or individual banishes itself, or its soul, which is its entity.

Reading 3744–4
[Background: From a series of readings on psychic phenomena]

(Q) *Is the Darwinian theory of evolution of man right or wrong? Give such an answer as will enlighten the people on this subject of evolution.*

(A) Man was made in the beginning, as the ruler over those elements as was prepared in the earth plane for his needs. When the plane became that such as man was capable of being sustained by the forces and conditions, as were upon the face of the earth plane, man appeared not from that already created, but as the Lord over all that was created, and in man there is found that in the living man, all of that that may be found without in the whole, whole world or earth plane, and *other* than that, the *soul of man* is that making him above all animal, vegetable, mineral kingdom of the earth plane.

Man *did not* descend from the monkey, but man has evolved, resuscitation, you see, from time to time, time to time, here a little, there a little, line upon line and line and line upon line.

In all ages we find this has been the developing—day by day, day by day, or the evolution as we see from those forces as may be manifested by that, that man has made himself the gradual improvement upon the things made by man, yet made to suffice the needs of certain functioning portions of man's will force, as may be manifested by man, but ever remaining that element to supply that need, whether of sustenance or other functions of man's individual needs, as created by man, this becoming then the exponent of the force as his Creator made him, for the world, and the needs and conditions, man's compliance nearer with those laws brings him gradually to that development necessary to meet the needs of the conditions, place or sphere in which that individual is placed. As in this:

The needs of those in the north country not the same as those in the torrid region. Hence development comes to meet the needs in the various conditions under which man is placed. He only using those laws that are ever and ever in existence in the plane, as is given in that of relativity, that being the needs from one relation to another.

The theory is, man evolved, or evolution, from First Cause in creation, and brings forth to meet the needs of the man, the preparation for the needs of man has gone down many, many thousands and millions of years, as is known in this plane, for the needs of man in the hundreds and thousands of years to come. Man is man, and God's order of creation, which he represents even as His son, who is the representative of the Father, took on the form of man, the highest of the creation in the plane, and became to man that element that shows and would show, and will show the way, the directing way, the life, the water, the vine, to the everlasting, when guided and kept in that manner and form.

(Q) *Where does the soul come from, and how does it enter the physical body?*

(A) It is already there. "And He breathed into him the breath of life, and he became a living soul," as the breath, the ether from the forces as come into the body of the human when born breathes the breath of life, as it becomes a living soul, provided it has reached that developing in the creation where the soul may enter and find the lodging place.

All souls were created in the beginning, and are finding their way back to whence they came.

(Q) *Where does the soul go when fully developed?*

(A) To its Maker.

4

●

Soul Development

Reading 136–83

(Q) *Now, is it possible for the ego to return to the physical plane again, except through the route of the cradle?*

(A) That dependent not only upon the mental and spiritual desire of the ego, but also upon the desire of those who study those impressions that are not effaced in the earth. These made one, may bring into being that of the entity in such a manner as to be made, to be seen, felt, heard, and in such there becomes oft danger unless understood. In this is the physical as one set in motion those of the spiritual force, as is made manifest in each entity, or so in body; this as it moves from sphere to sphere, seeks its way to the home, to the face of the Creator, the Father, the First Cause, the All–Infusible Force as is manifest; as the ties of sphere to sphere recede, then self is lost in that of attaining for itself the nearer and nearer approach that buildeth in manifested form, whether in the Pleiades, Arcturus, Gemini, or in earth, in Arcturus, Vulcan, or in Neptune, and seeks to draw that as is experienced through the sphere, passing, then, ever as light, a ray that does not end, lives on and on, until it becomes one in essence with the source of light. Same as the entity this so moves sphere to sphere. Have you not read of: "Know Ye Not, That Ye Must Be Born of Water and of the Spirit?" The water in material, the Mother of life, the Spirit, the Father, or that moving to bring life. Is it possible, then, that a man when he is old, shall again enter his mother's womb and be born again? He must be born of water and of blood. Blood, a manifestation of force that through which life manifests in its various forms. Water, the cleansing force as one moves from experience to experience.

Reading 212–1

(Q) How can this body improve her spiritual standing for her body's interest?

(A) Understand self and self's impulses. Then there may be seen that necessary for the conditions that may need correction or change; for each condition in a life, physical, mental or spiritual, must be met. Delay only makes the conditions the harder to meet.

Reading 238–2

In entering the present experience we find, astrologically, the entity coming under the influence of Jupiter, Mercury, Venus and Uranus. In the application of the entity and the experience in the earth's plane, these would be found to mean little, were they judged astrologically alone; for often do the experiences in the various phases of development, through the experiences in the various spheres, bring the varied *effect*, as is applicable to an individual in the application of its own will. Not that will is ever taken from an individual entity, but that builded in each experience must be met *by* that entity, and only in making self's own will one *with* the divine Creative Energy, and becoming as one with same, may one develop in any experience; and in *this* entity many developments and many retards are seen.

Reading 243–10

One that is in that position of making friends easily, and just as easily losing same; yet there are friendships made that make for the better understanding in the experience, and in those of *Venus* forces comes the love that is *innate* in the experience of the entity. Through all the vicissitudes of life this remaineth, for the entity has gained much that makes for that as was given—"There is a friend that sticketh closer than a brother," and "He that is just kind to the least of these, my little ones, is greater than he that hath taken a mighty city." These building, these kept within the consciousness of the entity, will build to that Christ Consciousness as makes all free; for in Him is the life, and He is the light that shineth into the dark places, even to the recesses of that of His own consciousness that makes for that which casteth out fear; (for being afraid is the first consciousness of sin's entering in, for he that is made afraid has lost consciousness of self's own heritage with the Son; for we are heirs through Him to that kingdom that is beyond all of that that would make afraid, or that would cause a doubt in the heart of any. Through the recesses of the heart, then, search out that that would make afraid, casting out fear, and *He* alone may guide).

Reading 254–68

(Q) *Submitted by Rev. W. [Presbyterian minister]: What, where or how is the direct and immediate point of contact between the personal God and the soul, of which contact the soul is conscious and certain?*

(A) As the sons and daughters of God are personal, are individual, with their many attributes that are characteristics, personalities or individualities, so (as this then is a shadow from that from which it sprang, its Maker) must the Maker be individual, with its attributes and its personalities. And yet fill all of life as becomes manifested in the spiritual realm, the realm of the soul or the temporal house, the abode of the soul for a day.

As the soul seeks, then, for that which is the sustenance of the body—as what the food is to a developing, a growing body, so are the words of truth (which are life, which are love, which are God) sought that make for growth, even as the digesting of the material things in a body make for a growth. This growth may not be felt in the consciousness of materialization. It is experienced by the consciousness of the soul, by which it enables the soul to use the attributes of the soul's food, even as the growth of the body makes for the use of the muscular forces or attributes of the physical body.

Where is the contact?

As ye seek Him, so does like beget like. For, ye are co–laborers with Him, if ye have put on the whole of His love in thine own life.

Feed, then, upon the fruits of the spirit. Love, hope, joy, mercy, long-suffering, brotherly love, and the contact, the growth, will be seen; and within the consciousness of the soul will the awareness come of the personality of the God in thee!

Reading 257–123

(Q) *Please advise me as to my spiritual development or retardment during 1933.*

(A) This may be best done within self, in the manners that have oft been outlined for self; in that: When ye enter into the inner self and approach the Throne of grace, mercy, love, hope, is there within self that which would hinder from offering the best or seeking the best from that Throne of grace?

Doesn't it then become necessary that such hindrances be first laid aside? even as given of old? When thou bringest thine sacrifice, expecting to receive from that Throne of grace the mercy and hope desired, hast thou shown mercy? hast thou shown love? hast thou shown consideration in the activities, the associations of each and every individual, whether friend or foe?

For, God is no respecter of persons; but rather:

He that showeth himself forward, to him He is forward. He that showeth himself little, to him He becomes little (within his own self). In the same manner that an individual shows himself worthy or unworthy does the result come in the conscious activity of self.

For, as given to self often, know thyself and what thou believest; and to *whom* thou wouldst turn for the aid, counsel and guidance.

For, a few years in this mundane sphere is little compared to eternity.

Be not impatient with those even that would hinder thee from gaining something of the world's pleasures; but know, he that seeks to do the biddings of the Creative Forces in a manner that is constructive, gratifies that which is the *soul's* development.

For, the soul seeks growth; as truth, as life, as light, *is* in itself. God *is*, and so is life, light, truth, hope, love. And those that abide in same, grow. Those that abide in the shadow of the night, or the conditions that become or make for the fruits of these, do not grow.

Reading 262–24

(Q) *"All great things are slow of growth."*

(A) Just true! For, as has been given oft, the soul grows upon that it is fed. The soul of man is the greatest, then, of all creation, for it may be one with the Father. Little by little, line upon line, here a little, there a little—these are the manners of growth, that this may be one with Him. Lose not that as was given by Him, the greater of all those who gave the truths, that not only one *with* Him but individual in self! Not the whole, but equal *with* the whole—for one with Him. Ye, then, are not aliens—rather the *Sons* of the Holy One.

Reading 263–4

The entity was among those who joined with the Ibex rebellion, making for those associations and connections that later held out for longer activities against the return of the priest or the activities of the king during that experience. The entity lost and gained during the experience, for with the beginnings of those clean sings in the temples, with the rejuvenation of the priest and those activities of individuals that made for the ingatherings of those that these tenets might be taught to others in all the various activities, the entity became among the first as a *trained* nurse. And in this sojourn could the entity have made for itself a life of service in a manner that would have been excelled by few. This required self-sacrifice; this the entity from other experiences of sojourn did not make. These may be developed in self in such ways and manners in the present as to bring an advancement and a development in this experience.

Reading 264–31

Then the entity was well-balanced in body, in mind, and a helpmeet or aide to those in that particular vicinity and environ—until one that came through the land, in the name Bainbridge, led the body far astray in its moral and spiritual intent in the experience; and there came troubles by grudges, by being in the position of not considering self as being led but constantly blaming the body's associate for the troubles in mind, in body, in associations, and for the happenings that came in the experience.

However, in the latter portion—when there was the weighing together of the tenets that came from the influence in the experience of the body's companion in the present, towards those things pertaining to mental, material and spiritual laws—the entity calmed, and gained through the experience, bringing much to the development of self because of the experience.

In the present much of the associations of that experience weigh upon the mental, physical and spiritual influences of the body; as may be seen by self in analyzing same.   .

Reading 264–45

In giving that which may be helpful at this time, may there come with the awareness of the conscious mind, through the spiritual message that may be given, that in applying spiritual lessons to material facts there is the necessity that the body-mind and the soul-mind be at-one.

There have been, as indicated for the body, those periods of mental and spiritual developments for this entity; also those periods when the misapplication for the better development of the physical body has occurred, yet these should be looked upon as that which is necessary for the experience of the soul that these may be indeed one. For the awareness makes for first the *correct* attitudes of the soul-mind, of the conscious-mind of an entity, that resentment in *any* phase is but as a barrier for the more perfect development of the whole or of the soul. Also that gentleness, kindness, a soft word even when there is anger and resentment; when there are those feelings that arise from *any* experience that find expressions in sharpness of words, in a resentment in any manner, that but make such conditions that the whole becomes as but fear and trembling.

That there may be more awareness in the physical forces of the body, keep that constant building from within, making the conscious mind, the soul-mind, more and more with that oneness of purpose, or desire, and the expressions of same will be more in keeping with constructive, creative development in the self and in that the self gives out.

Reading 264–45

(Q) *What are my abilities in my innate and soul self which are latent, and how may I develop and use them rightly?*

(A) Again and again has this been given the body. The abilities of analyzing those that have the same rebellious influences in their lives, of their experiences, to this or that measure. And as the body-mind, as the soul-mind, as the entity enables others, so does it enable self to see, to know, that from every phase of experience which makes more and more aware of the spiritual import and to give the proper evaluation and interpretation of mental and soul activity in a body.

Is the motivative force of soul or spirit in growth in any manner, any *more* expressive of the God-influence in one element than another? All show forth His handiwork. Man alone, of self, through self, sets same aside for self-indulgences or self-aggrandizements, and gives then the improper evaluations here and there. But if the entity will seek and seek, more and more will the light of His love purify the body, the mind, and the growth of the soul be assured.

Reading 275–11

In the one before this we find in the land of the present nativity, and during those stirring periods when there were the raids and the invasions of those peoples who would dislodge the settlers in this new land, while the entity of the native—or of those born to the first settlers, and in the name Zangrill. In this experience the entity gained in many manners, especially as to the abilities to apply the hand to that of decorating, sewing, and of knitting or spinning, and such of those things that pertain to the crude manner of the preparing of apparel are especially interesting to the entity. In this experience the entity gained in that as pertains to the religious influence. Not from purely that of the imaginative, but as *well* that as is *builded* by the personal application of the relationships of individuals to other individuals; and to the entity, in this direction, it matters not the claims of one but the actions, to the entity, speak the influence as one may hold, or one may expect to influence the entity with. So, pretty speeches mean little to the entity—though the mannerisms *of* others influence the entity much.

In the one before this we find in that land now known as the Egyptian, and during that period [of Ra Ta] when there was the height of the first understanding—in an expressive manner—of man's relationships to his Maker and man's relationships to his fellow man. In that first school established as a curative and as a preventative, did the entity act in the capacity of an aide to those who ministered in this period. In the name Ai-Si. The entity gained through this experience, and many were the combinations of delicacies as were given to those recuperating from fevers, from injuries external in battle, and those various conditions that dealt with the developments of the *inner* man. The entity gained through this experience, and in the present that as may be applied in the same direction would be the field for development. Not until the entity has passed its twenty-eighth year should union, or those of the opposite sex relationships be oft considered—for those developments in body-mind, in body-physical, must in the present bring that to which the entity may attain, as in a life of *useful* service first being set, that the entity may gain the more in the present.

Reading 275-33

Hence the entity may in the present, when attuning self through its exercises in music, arouse within the inner self those latent abilities where there may be attunement with the soul, of the inner self that has been builded. For, as an individual attunes itself to that which it has attained even at a *moment* of time, there is aroused the abilities to *know* even that which *was* known through the experience . . .

(Q) *Is there any suggestion that will help entity in her progress of developing herself spiritually and psychically?*

(A) As we have indicated, as the entity turns more and more through music for the attuning of self (as music becomes the meditation period, the prayer period for the entity), the abilities to turn to the activities of Ai-Si become possible—as we have described.

Reading 423-3

As to the abilities in the present, and that to which it may attain, and how:

As has been seen from the experiences, whenever there have been those activities that have made for the exemplification of the so-called virtues in man's activities, there have been brought for the entity developments mentally, spiritually, in its relationships for its own soul's activity. For, only by aiding others may the soul within itself advance for its development towards filling that purpose for which it came into material experience in the earth (and as the entity finds, and as the entity seeks to know for what purpose it entered into this present sojourn in its present surroundings): That there might be manifest in the flesh those things in the mental and soul body that have been gained throughout the sojourns in the earth. For, only by manifested acts that make for a closer relationship of the soul to that source from which it sojourns, may there come the consciousness of self—and in self—being at an at-onement with the Creative Forces or God in the earth.

In the present, then, there are those abilities to influence groups, influence individuals, as to their proper relationships to the material conditions in the earth as related to their mental and soul development also, as well as to the more material things of life. Yet the greater joy, the greater development may come in making manifest those virtues that have been manifest in the earth by the entity in tolerance, in a closer sojourn of the manifesting of love and patience, and truth, and life, and light; for life and light are the manifestations of God in the earth.

Reading 476–1

In entering from the astrological aspects, or from the numerological aspects, we find these somewhat confusing—were a parallel drawn, or an application made of that which might be drawn from such purely astrological or numerological charts. Yet these forces and influences have much, or will have much to do in the experience of the entity during the present sojourn. The more the entity would comprehend the same, the more they may be used as stepping-stones in the application of self in its own entity and soul development.

In an experience in the earth's plane each soul should gain the knowledge of those forces, conditions or experiences that may influence an entity, a soul, the more. And not only have the knowledge or understanding of such influence but know that the influences are as guides, signposts, conditions. And the use of them may enable a soul to develop the more. For, what a body-mind, a soul-mind does about or with the knowledge or understanding that it has makes development for that soul. For, some beautiful comparisons may be drawn from the entity's own experiences in the earth. For, while the entity was an associate or a brother of Solomon in an experience, what one did with his knowledge and understanding and what the other did with his understanding made for quite a difference in each one's position in that experience and the sojourns of each soul in other experiences.

From the astrological aspects we find these as urges rather than impelling, but the inclinations and influences are constantly arising in the experience of the entity; and as to what the entity may do with such urges remains within the ken or realm of the entity to make or to mar its own soul development.

Reading 480-47

(Q) Can you tell me what is the best approach through this channel for me to gain an understanding from the spiritual angle of the apparent tragedy which has come in my life through the loss of my mother?

(A) The Lord giveth, the Lord taketh away. Such as these appear to come as trite sayings, but as we study the Scripture and the promises therein, we find that only does the answer come within the self. Know that as He *wills*, only that which is for the individual—for *all* concerned—the will of Him as it is done in each, able to make for that an awakening necessary for the better understanding.

Condemning of self, of others, of the lack of this or that or the other, only creates barriers that make for the *inability of* the self to catch the glimpse.

Read that which has been indicated in the last admonition of Moses, in the 30th of Deuteronomy. Read of those promises in the Psalms—as in the 24th, the 23rd, the 91st, the 1st, the 150th. All of these will indicate that which is the *source* of strength mentally and spiritually, and—if we coordinate our mental and physical selves—also the source of our body's strength. For, as indicated in those, the *source* of all is there.

If we look, then, for other means—or material means—for the answer, there is none. Only is it found in Him.

Reading 488-6

(Q) Is entity holding right ideals for its spiritual development?

(A) As indicated by that given, that—will the entity hold that same attitude, that same willingness to be shown—there will be presented, there will be gradually builded; for that we think upon, that we become—for "where the treasure is, the heart is also." That which *is* a body's, an entity's, ideal, by that the standard of moral, mental and spiritual aptitudes, by that same classification comes the experiences of a body-consciousness. That there are builded in many an entity that innate prejudice against certain things or conditions, may be oft seen manifest—but the *willingness*, the surrender of self that self may be a channel of blessings, not to any force, or source, but to God! and for *Creative* Forces to manifest *through!* this is the attitude for an entity to take. *Walk* with Him! *Talk* with Him! See *Him* as He manifests in every form of life; for He *is* Life in *all* its manifestations in the earth! and there will come that peace, that harmony, that understanding, that comes from *humbleness* in *His* name; humbleness of spirit, of mind, of self, that the glories that are thine own *from* the foundations of the earth may be manifested *in* thee!

(Q) *Give spiritual advice to guide entity through college.*

(A) Be well to hold to that just given. *Know* the ideal. Measure the moral life, the social life, the material life, the spiritual life, by that standard. Lose not sight of that thou believest. *Know* in what thou hast believed, and be willing to be guided by *that* as the standard; for He *made* the earth—and all that in it be! In Him we live and move and have our beings! That we may separate elements, compounds, the various forces in nature, into their various parts, only becomes the more proof of not the *divisibility* of God! but that the *source* of force *and* power is *in* Him alone, and that individuals are but the reflection of their concept of that force that may be manifested in so many ways and manners in a material world! Lose not that hope in Him!

Reading 517–1

From Mercury we find the natural high intellectual activities of the entity, and the abilities in the present for not only retaining but for analysis of those things that pertain to the mental influences or environs of the entity.

Jupiter, in its broader aspect of all the attributes of human emotions, has made for the ability of the entity not only as a writer, in the application of itself as respecting sojourn or travel or change, change of environs, but the broad aspect of life in all of its attributes; and it is innate in the experiences and the abilities of the entity to make personal applications of these in the experience to the aid of self in the material and the aid of the mental and physical in others' experiences.

Also in Neptune there are brought the watery environs, and the associations with individuals who have had the more effectual activity in the experience of the entity are those who have recently been across large bodies of water, or who in their sojourns and in their relations one to another have had dealings with those who have recently been or who are engaged in activities that have to do with the water. There is also the interest in mystery, mystery stories, as well as those influences in things that are of the psychic nature. And, if the body applies its abilities as related to the visions in Jupiter and in Mercury *and* in Neptune, as in relation to that which may be given to others in their understanding or *application* of things pertaining to the mysteries of life—whether this be from the material, the mental or even the spiritual aspect—it will make for those channels through which the entity may give not only that which will be the more helpful but will also, in its application for others, find in self that which will bring to self the satisfaction that comes with the application of the mental influences and abilities in such a way and manner as to make for soul development. For, to the entity, it would require patience in these directions, and—as the teacher of old has given—"In patience possess ye your souls." This does not mean in bearing with individuals that willfully disobey, but rather being strong and steadfast and humble in the sight of higher forces, yet active in that known to be not only duty in the spiritual sense but duty in the mental and material sense. For, duty and patience are akin; for he that grows weary in well-doing, or who falters and faints and gives up, is not worthy of those things that may be his lot, or his niche or his channel in bringing to pass into the material manifestations those things that the higher influences—or even the angels of light—have had orders to prepare for those that love His ways.

Reading 537–1

The entity then was in the place known as Philadelphia, in the name Marjorie Akin; among those that rejoiced, as many rejoiced during that particular period. For, it was then in the heyday of life in the experience, and gave expression to self in the ways and manners as did many another; though of those peoples that were called Brethren or Quakers. And with and through those people did the entity give much that was helpful and hopeful; and even today there may be found something of the writings among those peoples in that particular vicinity, as to how the application of freedom was made; as the church; and what the better things stood for, that the entity gave for the young.

In the experience the entity gained through the greater portion, and those things that are innate as for the abilities to speak well, and to express self well in those things that pertain to helpful or hopeful influences in the lives of others, were manifested. . .

There are those things of specific natures, as we have indicated, to which the entity may lend itself; and thus bring development for self. Also in preparing, writing or dictating or presenting stories for children in such manners that they may be used in their studies, in their gaining the proper training and development in their spiritual life. In this field of activity the entity may not only find contentment but soul development; making, of course, the practical application from the experiences in Galilee, Judea, Capernaum; also that which has loosened peoples' minds in the various periods of removal of oppression and given them free thought in manifesting their expressions, their activity for the love of Creative Forces, or God.

Reading 610–1

(Q) *Please advise me and give me such guidance necessary to protect my present investments, and warnings to prevent possible errors in the future.*

(A) Again would we give the greater basis that that which may be given as warning that this will rise and that will fall.

God ever gives the increase. For, when the purposes in life and the desires of the heart and the mind, soul and body—are made in accord, "all these things shall be added unto you." What was the variation in that Abraham gave from the rest of the world? That the Lord thy God is One? The Lord thy God is *one* in thee! Thy mind, thy soul, thy body being one in purpose, in aim, in desire, He will lead thee in the ways that He will open—even the oneness of heaven, to pour into thine understanding that which will bring the greatest development of thy soul.

Put not thy trust in things that are of the earth-earthy, but rather in the promises that are sure, that He gives that necessary day by day; and as to whether ye shall sell or invest, whether ye shall trade or whether ye shall gather more and more, this will be shown thee—for thou art sensitive in thine self! Ye have received them rather as hunches, but "Inasmuch as ye do it unto the least, ye do it unto me." And He will show thee the way.

Reading 619-5

The Mercurian influences make for the high mental abilities or mental efficiency, coupled with the Jupiterian and Uranian influences. Hence while the entity may flare at some point, almost immediately it is as but the *deeper* self saying, "Let's reason together," as it were. Not that there is not temper, not that there is not the expression of same; but rather from the developments of the soul in the environs there has been brought into the experience of the entity in the earth *one* of the seven virtues, that may be said to stand equal to or ahead of them all—*tolerance,* and patience! Not that there are not those feelings otherwise and the giving of expression to same; for these from the earthly sojourns—it will be seen—become rather as emotions. But when the deeper self or the real development of the entity in the earthly sojourn finds expression, it becomes rather as it may be said or was said of many of old, that his tolerance, his patience, is counted for righteousness unto him that manifests in this body . . .

Before this we find the entity was in not the land of the present nativity, but in the land of the present sojourn. For the more often in the experience it will be found that the expressions and the activities are those drawn from one experience to another, for those individual developments or expansions of activity—and its innate and manifested abilities in the earth.

During that sojourn, then, we find the entity was in the land in and about what is now known as Dearborn, or Fort Dearborn; during those experiences when there were the gatherings of peoples from what was then called Lorraine, or the French peoples or immigrants—but of the same faith as in the present.

Then, the entity's activities were in the dealings or tradings with the natives of the north land, those of the western lands; not only for the pelts or skins or furs, but in the exchange of the fruits of the lands that were to be used by those peoples in or around those portions of the lakes—or around the forts established near what is now called Cleveland. And between these did the activities of the entity, in its active years, make for a development, for a growth, then in the name of Samuel Goldestenblenut.

In the experience the entity gained; for those dealings with the natives made for the establishings of the better relationships, even when there were those turmoils between the English and the French during those periods when the entity was the more active in those tradings.

Yet some misjudged the entity's principles, misjudged the entity's activities. And it brought a period of distress for the entity. Yet as there were the re-establishings of those activities that made for the greater progress, or the advancing of those that made this land become progressive in homes and trading, the entity grew to be one in power. And thus gained the more in making for harmonies in the relationships of the natives as well as those who pushed forward toward those settlings in the land during those periods.

Reading 640-1

Even though an entity in the earth's plane, in this life, may reach the years of fourscore and ten, these are as but moments in eternity. How oft would it be the better that each soul weigh those things in its experience that it knows! and to consider that someone cares; for He, the Lord of light, the way, the truth, the bright and morning star, the lily of the valley, the rose of Sharon, awaits—and has given His angels charge concerning thee, that thou walkest in the light. Be patient; for in patience, in waiting on the Lord, in being kind and gentle, do ye become aware of His presence in the earth. Not unto vaingglorying, but be ye joyous in the service that would make of thee—in thy temptations, in thy trials—as one that would be a bright and morning star, a hope to thy fellow man, a prop to those that falter and stumble, a refuge to those that are troubled in body and mind!

Reading 694–2

Then we find not only the influences from the astrological sojourns but from the material environments of the entity under such conditions where there were given, as it were, by those environs in which the entity enacted its sojourns in the earth, the accrediting of activities in the associations of that sojourn, that have builded for omens, the numerological, those that are often called the superstitions of the people in the various environs. Hence we find these as those things that should be in the form of omens about the body; not as good luck charms, but they may be termed so by many; for these are from those activities and sojourns that will make for variations in the *vibrations* about the entity, hence bringing much more of harmony into the experience of the entity in the present activity: The very red stones; as of coral, that is rather of the deep sea variety, and when this is worn about the neck or about the waist—or upon the arm—let it rest upon the flesh, for it will bring quiet to the body. Let the raiment be something of blue, *ever*, upon the flesh of the body, whether in the waking or in the sleeping—and especially in the sleeping hours, for it will bring the influences as the music that quiets, through the vibrations that are set off by such. And let the numbers as in three, six and nine ever be the choice, whether in the activities in the material, in the sojourn, in the position, in the place, or in *whatever* the activities may be; for these carry with them their vibration by the *natural* relative forces to the human emotions. And the body will find that the unquiet and the tumultuous conditions will be changed to the harmonious abilities to give out. And if a body–mind, a body–physical, a soul–body would have understanding, then give—that it may have. For they that would have life, love, hope, faith, brotherly love, kindness, gentleness, mercy, must *show* these things in their relationships to those they meet in every walk of life. *Dare* to speak gently, when even thine self is troubled. Dare to speak gently when thou art even berated by those from whom, in the *material* sense, ye have every right to expect or to even demand honor, and hope, and faith. Though they act in the opposite, with these environs about self as intimated the entity will be able to meet such; not as omens, not as good luck, but as facts for thine *own* development. For thy soul has been tried as by fire through many of thine experiences in the earth. Yet there are those things that make for harmony in their relationships as one to another, as do the turmoils of the mother-water that brings forth in its activity about the earth those tiny creatures that in their beginnings make for the establishing of that which is the foundation of much of those in materiality. Hence the red, the deep red coral, upon thine flesh, will bring quietness in those turmoils that have arisen within the inner self; as also will the pigments of blue to the body bring the air, the fragrance of love, mercy, truth and justice that is within self.

Reading 696–3

(Q) *Convinced that my present life's work is inspirational writing, I desire to know what specific course I should follow in life in order to gain more experience which will give me further deep insight into my fellow man's needs.*

(A) As illustrated by that given, the power comes in giving the expression of the inner self, letting the soul manifest, letting the self—the personality of self—become less and less in its desires, letting His desire be the ruling force. As He gave out, so was the power, the ability, the experience His that He *is*, He *was*, He *ever will be* the expression, the *concrete* expression of *love* in the minds, the hearts, the souls of men.

Then, broaden thy field of activity. Fear not to approach thy observations in columns even of the secular world; as the *Christian Herald* or *Christian Advocate*, or the *Sunday School Times*. For the more and more that ye have the body of many giving praises and thanks for the hope that ye create in their minds and their hearts, greater is the experience and the *ability* of expression. For the law, the love holds as He gave; one may cry aloud and long for *self* and yet *never* be heard, but where two or three are gathered in His name there is He in the midst of them. So, as ye give out is the power received. Do not understand that ye may not enter into thine own closet and there meet thy Savior within, but—as given—when ye cry for *self*, and *self* alone, ye close the door, ye stand as a shadow before the altar of thy god within thyself.

Give, then, in broader fields of activity, in *every* channel where those that are seeking may find; that are wandering, that are lame in body, lame in mind, halt in their manner of expression, that are blind to the beauties in their own household, their own hearts, their own minds. These thou may awaken in all thy fields. And as ye do, greater is thy vision—and He will guide thee, for He hath given His angels charge concerning those that seek to be a channel of blessing to their fellow man; that purge their hearts, their bodies, of every selfish motive and give the Christ—*crucified, glorified*—a place in its stead.

Reading 752-1

For, not only through its sojourns in the earth but in the environmental influences about the earth, the entity has gained the virtues of patience and tolerance. If these are kept in that same attitude in which the entity has thus far experienced in its application of that it has attained respecting the Creative Forces in the material and in the mental world, they will bring happiness and joy in the very activities that will shut away, will mark from the entity's experience all of sorrow and sadness. For, as has been given, he that loveth his brother may indeed through patience become aware of his soul and its activity in even material things. For the entity having endured even from the beginnings may know, even as He has given.

Reading 792-2
[Background: From a reading on psychic development]

(Q) *Please suggest the type of experiments which may be conducted most successfully by this group.*

(A) Well, you would have to take each as an individual—to say as to which may be the most successful! For there are grades, there are variations. There are in the group, as has been indicated, curiosity, wisdom, folly, *and* those things that make for real spiritual development. They each then require first—first—self-analysis! *What* prompts the individual to seek, engage, or desire to join in such experiments? As to how far, as to what—there is no end! Is there any end to infinity? For this is the attunement, then—to Infinity!

Each will find a variation according to the application and the abilities of each to become less and less controlled by personality, and the more and more able to shut away the material consciousness—or the mind portion that is of the material, propagated or implied by what is termed the five senses. The more and more each is impelled by that which is intuitive, or the relying upon the soul force within, the greater, the farther, the deeper, the broader, the more constructive may be the result.

More and more, then, turn to those experiments that are not only helpful but that give hope to others, that make for the activity of the fruits of the spirit.

Make haste slowly.

Wait on the Lord; not making for a show, an activity of any kind that would be self–glorification, self–exaltation, but rather that which is helpful, hopeful for others.

Reading 858–1

Before this we find the entity was in the earth during those early periods of activity in the land of present nativity, but rather in and about those environs that were called "the brethren," or about what is now known as the "city of brotherly love," or Philadelphia.

There we find the entity was among the earlier individuals that came into the experience in that land; and in the name then of Edith Connell, the entity was very demure, very shy, gaining much through the experiences in those lessons of patience. Although in the earlier portion of the young womanhood the entity *rebelled* much, it aided in that which later became in this country, in this new land, the writing, the engraving, the bookmarks, bookmaking. The entity's activities were in the application of printing in its forms of the period. Being subjugated as to its associations with the opposite sex, the entity turned itself to the crafts of the day; and in those expressions it found an activity, later making for those associations in which it may be said that the entity indeed had an experience worthy of a great soul. For even though turmoils and strifes arose, in the experience of those round about, that gentleness of the experience brought for the entity a contentment, a harmony that was not well understood by many.

Yet it makes for in the present experience its friendships, of the entity, as those that are chosen; rather than being chosen by others.

Reading 900–16

(Q) *Explain the various planes of eternity, in their order of development, or rather explain to us the steps through which the soul must pass to climb back into the arms of beloved God.*

(A) These, we see, must be manifest only as the finite mind in the flesh. As in the spirit forces, the development comes through the many changes, as made manifest in the evolution of man.

In the development in eternity's realm, is that a finite force as made of creation may become one with the Creator, as a unit, atom, or vibration, becomes one with the universal forces. When separated, as each were in the beginning, with the many changes possible in the material forces, the development then comes, that each spirit entity, each earth entity, the counterpart of the spirit entity, may become one with the Creator, even as the ensample to man's development through flesh, made perfect in every manner; though taking on the flesh, yet without spot or blemish, never condemning, never finding fault, never bringing accusation against any, making the will one with the Father, as was in the beginning. For, without passing through each and every stage of development, there is not the correct vibration to become one with the Creator, beginning with the first vibration, as is of the spirit quickened with the flesh, and made manifest in material world (earth's plane).

Then, in the many stages of development, throughout the universal, or in the great system of the universal forces, and each stage of development made manifest through flesh, which is the testing portion of the universal vibration. In this manner then, and for this reason, all made manifest in flesh, and development through the eons of time, space, and *called* eternity.

(Q) *Now give this body, [900], that information which will lead him, when in communion with his God, and when in vision while asleep, to the knowledge of why the soul was fated to enter into all these experiences in order to develop of its own free will to perfection, and then return to God, when God first created souls in a perfect state. Was it to force the spirit to choose with its will the righteous path to God, in spite of any circumstances and conditions? Was it to see if that which once [was] created perfect would return to the perfect? Explain and illustrate.*

(A) This we find has been given, and is manifest in the life of the lowly Nazarene. As has been given, man was made a little lower than the angels, yet with that power to become one with God, while the angel remains the angel.

In the life, then, of Jesus we find the oneness made manifest through the ability to overcome all of the temptations of the flesh, and the desires of same, through making the *will one with the Father.* For as we find, oft did He give to those about him those injunctions, "Those who have seen me have seen the Father," and in man, He, the Son of Man, became one with the Father. Man, through the same channel, may reach that perfection, even higher than the angel, though he attend the God.

Reading 903-23

For a moment, let's turn to what *is* that termed as the Akashic Record, or that which may be said to be destiny in the entrance of a soul into materiality. For remember, matter moved upon—or matter in motion in materiality—becomes the motivative force we know as the evolutionary influence in a material world. An entity or soul is a portion of the First Cause, or God, or Creative Energy; or the terms that may be had for the *movement* that brings matter into activity or being. Hence souls in their varied experiences—whether in the earth or materiality or in the various spheres of activity about the earth (termed the astrological sojourns and their influences, where there have been the fruits of what? Spirit! as the motivative forces in a contact)—are again and again *drawn* together by the natural law of attractive forces for the activity towards what? The *development* of the soul to the *one* purpose, the *one cause*—to be companionate with the *First Cause!*

Then as the entity here contacts in materiality those of its own body, those of its own sympathetic condition, it is for the development of each in its associations one to another toward that First Cause.

As to each of the children then, as we find, these have been leading one another, leading self, the ego, to these varied activities.

(Q) *Does the entity understand correctly that she has never been previously associated with her present children?*

(A) Not for their own soul and spiritual development. Materially, yes; in those activities, though, that made for *materiality* they came to the entity in those material associations. In this it is their *soul* development, see?

Keep, then, that opportunity that through the Creative Forces as in the astrological, the higher soul development from the material planes that are influencing the entity in the present, there may be such an at-oneness with that that there may be brought *this* awareness; that what is constructive in the influence of any soul is of the spiritual force or God influence—and that which makes for the separation of some is that which will weaken and sap the materiality in any soul.

Reading 909–1

Think never that the opportunities have passed; forever is there set before thee a choice to make, and has always been given *"Today* is the acceptable year, the acceptable day, of the Lord!" It is never too late to begin, even in an experience; for life in its experience is a continued, a continuous effort—in making, in starting, the associations which bring what has ever been given as the way whereby man may justify himself before the Throne of grace in a material world: "Inasmuch as ye do it unto the least of these, my little ones, ye do it unto me."

When there is, then, that activity whereunto there is made known more and more in the minds and hearts and experiences of all that whereunto they have been called for a purpose in a material manifestation, greater and greater becomes—and grows—the possibility, the capability, of advancement.

Reading 934–6

(Q) *If running the Stand, would the gain be material or spiritual?*

(A) Unless it is spiritual, mental *and* material, it is not a gain. And it may only be made a gain with first setting the standard *spiritually, mentally,* and the material the outcome of that activity—for that it will be.

For as has been indicated; the seed ye sow must be reaped; and that ye have *sown* will be reaped also. But meet it—in meekness, in faith, in determination to do the right for the right's sake, mentally and spiritually; and the material gain will be commensurate with the faith, the work, the activity given.

Reading 951–4

In the experience the entity gained through those periods when its activities were such as to induce individuals, or youth, to prepare themselves—in the physical as well as mental educations—for the bringing of others into the experiences to carry on.

Thus we find the entity acted in the capacity not so much as a social worker, nor yet as a school teacher, but rather as one who waited upon many through those associations with the companion, in ministering to the needs of the peoples in the communities.

In the present experience from same, then, we find the ability to establish the home—as well as to be an instructress for the development of body, in recreation as well as for poise, for manner, for speech; and in such physical activity becomes the *natural* outlet for the entity in the present.

Hold fast, ever, to *everything* that is creative, constructive, and of spiritual import.

Reading 954–4

Study those that have been given as the faults, as the failures, as the weaknesses, as the virtues, as the goodness.

For there is in the experience of every entity so *much* good that they who find faults to exalt them, or to rear them up as signs—they that do such make these become as the stumbling stones for themselves.

This does not proclaim then that one shall live only a passive life, but rather a positive life—in the *doings* of self! For it is not what one knows that counts but rather what one does about that one knows! For it is line upon line, precept upon precept, here a little, there a little. For ye grow in grace and in knowledge and in understanding as ye apply that in thine experience that makes the paths straight, that keeps upon the way that is constructive in the experience.

Reading 1100–31

In respect to associations with varied individuals, or groups of individuals with which an entity has been associated—as these phases of one's experience are considered, it is well that there be the proper understanding as concerning the laws respecting time, place, and how individuals are naturally attracted in group activity. And no matter in what realm, or in what material place, those phases of experience where there has been an activity of an individual entity, either some individual or some phase of individuals' activities may be met.

While the problems to be met are not always with the same individual entities, they are relatively worked out as to their varied positions in respect to the prompting influence or urge of the entity through such an experience.

Then, we would give an illustration to the entity of such associations—also as to the universal laws that bring about the relative relationships under varied circumstance:

What an entity sows, that it reaps. In relation to what? That chosen in the experience as the ideal of the entity, *and* the relationship such knowledge or such an ideal has to the First Cause or Premise—or God; according to how true, or how well in keeping with those ideals, one applies self.

Each entity must answer for its *own* choosing, as well as for those it—as an entity—has persuaded or prompted in certain directions.

For, it is true—physically, mentally or spiritually—that if the blind lead the blind, *both* will fall into the ditch.

In the experiences of meeting individuals and groups—as the entity has experienced through the present contacts or associations—certain urges arise emotionally, mentally and spiritually from sojourns in the earth, and these have been a part of the experience because of associations with individual entities; whether these were purely material associations, mental associations or spiritual associations.

The spirit alone keeps alive. The material, that is of the earth–earthy, passes with the earth, yet leaves its mark upon the individual entity—rather than upon a group; though individuals are grouped as associates again because of an urge of a complex or compound nature, or because of a universal urge.

Thus the necessity for choosing the spiritual ideal, in relationship to the Creative Forces—the First Cause, the First Premise, or God.

Then, in the light of these, the entity may study, understand and comprehend, as it meets or is associated with varied individuals.

For instance, the associations it has experienced with the present companion. Not that you each think as the other, or that you both think alike, but you each are the complement to the other in the material, the mental and the spiritual aspirations and desires; not wholly the same, but complementary one to the other.

Thus from the material angle the associations become ideal. In comparing the experiences of each through the earthly sojourns there may be indicated the periods of closer association in the material sense, in which there were those phases of advancement, development as comparable one to the other in spiritual, mental and physical attributes.

Thus the oneness as evidenced in the present associations.

Using such as a criterion, as a measuring stick, then—by comparison there may be understood the various associations of purposes and ideals of individuals as compared to self. And almost from the associations with the companion it may be understood at what period there must have been an association, or a material, mental or spiritual attraction that has brought an association in the present material sojourn.

Reading 1150–1

Remember, ever, that where shortcomings have existed and do exist in the experience, those that are wise use same as stepping–stones to the real development; for less and less of self, more and more that the body, the mind, may be used as a channel for the glorifying of a unified Father in the earth.

These should be, must be, the purposes, the aims, the desires for each soul if it would fulfill that whereunto it has been called into the earth.

That the earth has been given as a schooling for those that in the beginnings erred in self–indulgences, self–aggrandizement, self–glorification, is indeed a merciful experience then, even to those that find turmoils, strife and antagonism and disturbing forces in their experience. If they will but empty themselves of themselves, they may become channels through which a *glorified* Father *in* the Son may be manifested in and among men.

Reading 1175–1

(Q) How may I develop a spiritual consciousness, so as to make emotionally mine the belief that the so-called dead are alive; that my loved ones are near, loving me and ready to help me?

(A) As has been given, know thy Ideal, in what thou hast believed; and then act in that manner, ministering to others. For perfect love casteth out fear, and fear can only be from the material things that soon must fade away.

And thus hold to the higher thought of *eternity.* For life is a *continual* experience. And thy loved ones, yea those thou hast loved. For what draweth thee nigh to others, to do a kindly deed; to pass a kindly word to those that are disconsolate, those that are in sorrow? It makes for a bond of sympathy, a bond of love that surpasseth all joy of an earthly nature.

Reading 1242–6

(Q) *Any other advice for this body, either physical or spiritual?*

(A) There should be kept, to be sure, a hopeful, constructive attitude as to its material and physical welfare, as well as in its spiritual application and spiritual attitudes. For each soul should gain that understanding that whatever may be the experience, if there is not resentment, if there is not contention, if there is not the giving of offense, it is for then that soul's own understanding, and will build within the consciousness of the soul itself that which may bring the greater understanding of the spiritual in the physical body.

Reading 1300–1

These experiences then that have shattered hopes, that have brought disappointments, that have produced periods when there seemed little or nothing in the material life—if they are used in the experience as stepping-stones and not as those things that would bring resentments, accusations to others, those influences that create discontent, we will find they will become as helpful experiences that may guide the entity, the bodily influences, into a haven that is quiet and peaceful.

Hence the necessity as is in the entity's whole experience, that the faith, the hope in a divinity that is *within* be held—that shapes the destinies of individual experiences in such a way that the opportunities that come into the lives of individuals are those things which if taken correctly make for the greater soul development.

Then, look not back upon those periods of exaltation but rather into the hopefulness of a future in this experience when a *home* may be established that is an ideal in miniature of that heavenly peace that is to every soul that keeps its face to the light; and looks not back upon those shadows of doubt and fear that bring so oft so much discouragement that one fails to know there is a Friend indeed that is mindful of *every* thought, act and deed of a soul. And He hath not willed that any should be fraught with the fears of despair but hath with each temptation, with each doubt and each fear prepared a way of escape; that those who remain faithful will come to know the way in a much more glorious manner.

Reading 1465-2

(Q) Is it probable or correct for me to receive money from him in this life?
(A) Correct and probable—very probable.

In the use of same, it becomes only an expression of appreciation and love. Use not for other than giving to others the beauty of the abilities of self to see the vistas of the mountaintops of joy, and life in an experience of service though it mean perhaps toil or strife, though it may mean sacrifices from the standpoint of those things that materially seem so a part of life.

But life is earnest, life is true—and that which each soul experiences is a part of that necessary, if it will be used as such and not looked upon as a drudge or as a hindrance.

Whom the Lord loveth He cherisheth, whom the Lord loveth He chastiseth, whom the Lord loveth He raiseth up to opportunities.

If ye have shown and do show thyself worthy, then ye become even as the Son that ye saw, that ye worshiped with—though ye be the sons, the daughters of the living God, yet learn ye—as the world, yea as the universe—obedience through suffering.

Reading 1472-3

For, as then, the evolution of man's experiences is for the individual purpose of becoming more and more acquainted with those activities in the relationships with the fellow man, as an exemplification, as a manifestation of Divine Love—as was shown by the Son of man, Jesus; that *each* and every soul *must become, must be*, the *savior* of some soul! to even *comprehend* the purpose of the entrance of the Son *into* the earth— that man might have the closer walk with, yea the open door to, the very heart of the living God!

Reading 1581–2

(Q) Which of my associates should I avoid and which should I cultivate to help me toward my own unfoldment?

(A) As has so oft been indicated here, and as has been the experience of the entity in that particular sojourn just indicated that was a period of great advancement in development, no associate *ever* becomes a part of thine experience save as an opportunity for the developing of that thou dost hold as thy ideal.

That there may be easier ways, by taking that which is the easier way, is evident—as ye grow in experience of application of self. But rather live thine own life, and use each associate, each opportunity as the means for giving expression to that which *is* thy ideal.

And then the fruits of thy activity will—even as with [Him]—cement those friendships that may bring the greater blessing in thine *own* experience, as well as in the experience of all whom ye contact.

There is no such thing as having too many friends, or having so many that you can afford to lose a single one.

This does not indicate, to be sure—as from what has just been given—that all are within the inner circle, as it were, but rather that ye will lose no opportunity—by mere acquaintance or by passing chance—of giving the opportunity for such to know what is thy ideal.

Cultivate those who bring thee strength in thy ideal, *not* in thy weaknesses or thy faults. For these ye know within thine own self, as ye meet them day by day.

Reading 1641–1

The purpose for the entrance of each soul into a material experience is for the development that it, the soul, may be a companion with the Creative Forces. For that purpose this entity, this soul—as all others—came into being; to be a companion with the Creator.

There is the knowledge, there is the understanding that flesh and blood may not inherit eternal forces or principles. Hence the soul and mental self must be the builder, and that to such a way and manner that it may enjoy or be at peace in the presence of that it has chosen and does choose as its directing force or guidance.

Know then in whom—yea in what ye have believed and do believe;

and know that the author of same must be able to keep what ye commit unto him against any experience that may arise in thy associations and activities with thy environs, thy fellow man, thy activities in *any* influence; whether in the material, the mental or the spiritual realm.

Then as ye know, then as ye have heard, then as ye have in part experienced—ye *have* an Advocate, an ensample, a way and manner that is set before thee! that has given thee away, a manner in which ye may approach all phases of thy activity; whether in the mental or the physical or the spiritual realm.

For only the soul lives on. That which had a beginning has an end. Thy soul is a part of the beginning and the end, and thus is one with the Creative Forces or God—if ye will so act in thy relationships with thy purposes, thy desires, as to make that body (with which the soul is clothed) as companionable with Him.

These are the purposes, these are the intents for which each soul comes, then, into those experiences and activities in a material world.

For He hath not willed that any soul should perish, but hath with every temptation prepared a manner, a way in which ye may know thyself and thy relationships to the Creative Forces—as ye may manifest same to thy fellow man.

Reading 1981-1

Know that it is not by chance that one enters a material experience; rather the combination of minds as would create the channel to be offered for the expression of a soul, and the soul seeks same because of those desires of the two making one—thus bringing the opportunity.

Thus, those environs may change; and those activities of individuals may be changed by those influences that appear to be without the scope or cope of man's activity. All of these are oft visioned by the soul before it enters, and all of these are at times met in tempering the soul.

For, remember, He hath not willed that any soul should perish, but hath with each temptation, with each experience offered a channel, a choice whereby the soul is enlarged, is shown that the choice brings it nearer, nearer yet, to that purpose for which expression is given of same in the material world; even as He, the way, the life, the truth, came into life in materiality that we, through Him might have the advocate with the Father, and thus in Him find the answer to every problem in material experience.

Reading 2056–2

(Q) Regarding his connection with . . . in view of that which seems to be afoot, what should this body do relative to his association with this company?

(A) Discontinue connection with any condition that to the body-consciousness is not in keeping with the best development of self or of others. Never well to do evil or any underhanded thing that individuals or groups may benefit materially from same. Rather live that life that *merits* the best through *service* given to others—for the laborer is ever worthy of hire, and the Lord hath given and hath established that, "He that walketh in the way of the just shall receive the fat of the land." Let the Lord be thy God, rather than position, power, or fame—for in service to Him may the heart find that satisfaction that comes with a life being *well* spent, and do not so act that self-condemnation enters into thine inmost self.

(Q) Give the body any other advice that would be in keeping for the best development for this body.

(A) Keep thine face toward the light, and the shadows will not bring fright—for fear is the beginning of all undoing. Keep the heart singing, and the Lord will raise thee up to *magnify* His promises to men through service to thine fellow man, for he that lends to the Lord lays up a store in that realm where thieves do not break through nor steal. Keep thine ways open, above censure, and *never* censure self.

Reading 2672–2

In the one before this we find among those who first came as those peoples who settled in that country now known as Pennsylvania. The entity was among those of that religious sect under Penn. Then in the name of Dunden, and the entity gained in that period through service as the teacher to the inhabitants and to those peoples who came as settlers, giving self in much the manner as should have been, and should be as yet, manifested in the earth's plane. In the urge as is seen—the love of outdoors, and of flowers, and of shrub, and by nature much of an apiarist.

Reading 2813-1

The entity should know that it has a body, it has a mind, and hopes it has a soul. For, deep and latent within is that desire, that hope for some sort of a future consciousness.

Know that if there is any hope for a future consciousness, there *has* been a consciousness before this present awareness. For, all that is has been, and all that is to be has been already; and God requires the best of every individual soul.

For, the manifestations of a soul in the earth are the opportunity to make self so aware—by the application of those attributes to which you accredit any divinity in thine *own* relationships with thy fellow man.

Thus may the entity reason, and in so reasoning apply self in that measure as to become aware of the full measure of thy relationship to thy Creator—through thy application of such tenets as ye accredit to Him, in thy relationships to thy fellow man today.

Reading 3744-3
[Background: From a series of readings on psychic phenomena]

(Q) Do the planets have an effect on the life of every individual born?

(A) They have. Just as this earth's forces were set in motion, and about it, those forces that govern the elements, elementary so, of the earth's sphere or plane, and as each comes under the influence of those conditions, the influence is to the individual without regard to the will, which is the developing factor of man, in which such is expressed through the breath of the Creator, and as one's plane of existence is lived out from one sphere to another they come under the influence of those to which it passes from time to time.

In the sphere of many of the planets within the same solar system, we find they are banished to certain conditions in developing about the spheres from which they pass, and again and again and again return from one to another until they are prepared to meet the everlasting Creator of our entire universe, of which our system is only a very small part.

Be not dismayed. God is not mocked. "Whatsoever a man soweth that shall he also reap."

In the various spheres, then, through which he must pass to attain that which will fit him for the conditions to enter in, and become a part of that Creator, just as an individual is a part of the creation now. In this manner we see there is the influence of the planets upon an individual, for all must come under that influence, though one may pass from one plane to another without going through all stages of the condition, for only upon the earth plane at present do we find man is flesh and blood, but upon others do we find those of his own making in the preparation of his own development.

As given, "The heavens declare the glory of God, and the firmament showeth His handyworks. Day unto day uttereth speech, night unto night sheweth knowledge." This from the beginning and unto the end.

Just in that manner is the way shown how men may escape from all of the fiery darts of the Wicked One, for it is self, and selfishness, that would damn the individual soul unto one or the other of those forces that bring about the change that must be in those that willfully wrong his Maker. It is not the man's doing. It is that which is done, or left undone, or that indifference toward the creation that makes or loses for the individual entity. Then, let's be up and doing—doing. "Be ye doers; not hearers only."

Reading 5030–1

Thus that needed most in the entity's present experience is for the entity to study self. What is thy ideal? What is thy God? What is that controlling thee? For instance, when you sleep what keeps your heart still beating? Is it true that in Him, the Father of light, God, ye live and move and have thy being? Or is it purely a physical phenomenon? Is God the Creator of heaven and earth and all that is therein, or did it happen of itself? Know what ye believe and know who is the author of thy beliefs; not just because you have been taught this or that by any man. They can only bring to your mind that already contained and all those influences which may add to or take from, according to what spirit or truth ye entertain. For truth maketh thee not afraid. Truth is truth everywhere the same, under every circumstance. It is creative. For light, the Christ, Jesus is the truth, is the perfect way. They who climb up some other way are thieves and robbers to their own better selves.

Reading 5749–14

**[Background: From a reading on the philosophy chapter of
There Is a River]**

(Q) *The fourth problem concerns man's tenancy on earth. Was it originally intended that souls remain out of earthly forms, and were the races originated as a necessity resulting from error?*

(A) The earth and its manifestations were only the expression of God and not necessarily as a place of tenancy for the souls of men, until man was created—to meet the needs of existing conditions.

(Q) *The fifth problem concerns an explanation of the life readings. From a study of these it seems that there is a trend downward, from early incarnations, toward greater earthliness and less mentality. Then there is a swing upward, accompanied by suffering, patience, and understanding. Is this the normal pattern, which results in virtue and oneness with God obtained by free will and mind?*

(A) This is correct. It is the pattern as it is set in Him.

(Q) *Is the average fulfillment of the soul's expectation more or less than fifty percent?*

(A) It's a continuous advancement, so it is more than fifty percent.

5

●

Find Yourself First

Reading 452–3

(Q) *Why is it so hard for me to decide my life's work?*

(A) That which has been chosen has proven in self a disappointment in self. The trouble lies in self, rather than in that which has been or may be chosen. First find self, self's relationships to that self would worship. Self or its God? Self or its fellow man? Self or those things that partake of the carnal forces that manifest in the earth? for as one manifests so is the reflection of that that is held as its ideal.

Reading 826–11

Mind is the builder, being both spiritual and material; and the consciousness of same reaches man only in his awareness of his consciousnesses through the senses of his physical being.

Then indeed do the senses take *on* an activity in which they may be directed in that awareness, that consciousness of the spiritual self as well as in the physical indulgences or appetites or activities that become as a portion of the selfish nature of the individual or entity.

It behooves the entity first in its premise then to know, to conceive, to imagine, to become aware of that which is its ideal.

Not that alone of the ideal condition of the body as in relationship to its appetites, its factors—yea, even its functionings, nor only the abilities of the mind to be in the physical manner directed in such a way or manner that it may bring that which is the answer to the desires of the flesh. But also, or *rather*, that which takes hold on those things that are eternal in not *only* their awareness, not only in their application, but in their body, yea in their mind, yea in their application!

For as is the awareness of the mental self, the Spirit of God—or Good—is never seen by the material man, ever; only the effects and the application of those factors in the experience of the individual are made aware by that it brings into the consciousness through the senses—yea of the body, the awareness of the mental self and the spiritual self.

And this kept as a part of the development, the growth, the activity of the entity as a whole, becomes then a well-balanced unit; an entity that *is* conscious of the influences of infinity through the finite forces that may be given in what has been expressed as of old, "As ye do it unto the least of these thy brethren, ye do it unto thy Maker."

How, then, may an entity become aware of those influences of that infinite force and power, an intelligence that is the ruling force of that ideal life as may be manifested by this entity in this individual experience?

When the mental self is loosened in the quietness of those periods when it would take cognizance of the influences about self, we find the mental as a vapor, as a gas (not that it is either, but as comparison) is loosened by the opening of the self through those centers of the body that arouse the awareness of the mental to the indwelling of the spiritual self that is a portion of and encased within self. And it, the energy, the influence—as the vapor, as the gas—rises to the consciousness within, to the temple of the motivative forces of the physical body.

It, that energy, seeks—by the natural law—that to which it has an affinity. Affinity is the ideal, then.

If that mental self, that portion of the Spirit is in accord with the divine will—by its application of its knowledge as to its relationships to the fellow man in the manners and purposes as indicated—there comes that consciousness, that awareness that His Spirit indeed beareth witness with thy spirit.

And indeed ye may then find that access, that consciousness of His abiding presence with thee that ye may carry on, ye may fulfill, ye may keep inviolate all promises that thou hast made to thy Maker; that He hath made to thee!

Thus it is through thine own self. For indeed thy body is the temple of the living God. It is the temple of thine own awareness. It is the temple of thine own conscious walk with Him.

And the application of that received there, then, in thy physical consciousness, physical mind—applied in thy relationships to those ye meet day by day—causes the growth to come.

Reading 2072–10

(Q) What is the note of the musical scale to which I vibrate?

(A) As we have indicated, Ah—This is not R, but Ah—aum, see? These are the sounds. Those that respond to the centers of the body, in opening the centers so that the kundalin forces arise to that activity through those portions of the body. Sound these, and ye will find them in thyself. They are the manners or ways of seeking.

For as ye have understood, if ye have read Him and His conversation with His friends, His disciples as respecting John—John was a great entity, none greater. And yet the least in the kingdom of heaven was greater than he. What meaneth this manner of speech?

They that have wisdom are great, they that have understanding as to the manner to *apply* same for the good of self *and* others—not for self at the expense of others, but for others—are in the awareness of the kingdom.

Thus, as to the note of thy body—is there always the response to just one? Yes. As we have indicated oft, for this entity as well as others, there are certain notes to which there is a response, but is it always the same? No more than thy moods or thy tendencies, *unless* ye have arisen to the understanding of perfect attunement.

When a violin or an instrument is attuned to harmony, is it out of tune when struck by the same motion, the same activity? Does it bring forth the same sound?

So with thy body, thy mind, thy soul. It is dependent upon the tuning—whether with the infinite or with self, or with worldly wisdom. For these, to be sure, become the mysteries of life to some—the mysteries of attuning. What seek ye? Him, self, or what? He is within and beareth witness.

The tone, then—find it in thyself, if ye would be enlightened. To give the tune or tone as Do, Ah—aum—would mean little; unless there is the comprehending, the understanding of that to which ye are attempting to attune—in the spiritual, the mental, the material.

There *is* music in jazz, but is there perfect harmony in same? There *is* harmony in a symphony, as in the voices as attuned to the infinite—a spirit and a body poured out in aid or the search for the soul.

There is no greater than that as may be expressed in that of, "O my son Absalom, my son, my son Absalom! would God I had died for thee, 0 Absalom, my son, my son!"

To what is this attuned? What *is* the note there?

That as of the realization of the lack of training the mind of the son in the way of the Lord, rather than in the knowledge of controlling individuals.

This, then, is indeed the way of harmony, the way of the pitch, the way of the tone. It is best sounded by what it arouses in thee—where, when, and under what circumstance.

Reading 2487–2

(Q) Any other advice at this time?

(A) As indicated before—first, in all considerations, know self and thine own ideal—spiritually, mentally, materially. Stress not one more than the other; but an idea without a spirit, or based upon spiritual ideals, is already dead—or is without life, and may be only as an automatic reaction.

Reading 2438–1

In the activities—first study self. Write down, make a list of what ye desire most. And as ye find each thing on thy list pertains to that as would gratify or satisfy personal self, replace same continuously with that wish expressed in these words—"Lord, use me in thine *own* way!" Thus we will find these of self will be gradually eliminated, and the awakening that comes from within taking its place.

For, know that the answer to every problem, to every question, is within self. For there, as given, He has promised to meet with thee.

Reading 830-3

Hence as has been given, *know* thyself, in *whom* thou believest! Not of earthly, not of material things, but mental and spiritual—and *why*! And by keeping a record of self—not as a diary, but thy purposes, what you have thought, what you have desired, the good that you have done—we will find this will bring physical and mental reactions that will be in keeping with the purposes for which each soul enters a material manifestation.

Reading 3106-1

While urges latent and manifested are indicated in the entity's experience, none of these surpass the birthright of each soul. For, the entity enters a material manifestation that it may show appreciation, that it may show the glory of the Creative Force or God in the earth. That should be its purpose, its aim, its desire.

When there is the manifestation—as there is the tendency in the experience of this entity—to show the own ego in self-indulgence in any form, this becomes as the setting up of some other gods before that which is the purpose through which life itself is maintained. And this may become a stumbling block in the material experiences in the earth.

For, there are those immutable, unchangeable laws. These are oft termed in the material world cause and effect, or—by some—karmic influences. Yet none of these, if the ideal is set, should separate the individual entity from the awareness of the Creative Forces' operation through its own experience.

As to the innate or so-called astrological influences, we find these apparent: Mercury, Jupiter, Saturn, Mars, Venus. These, in varied aspects, carry latent urges—or susceptibility of the consciousness of the entity's inner self. But the use or application depends upon what the entity has set as its ideal, and how consistently the entity applies same in the daily experience.

In the astrological urges we find the high mental abilities, the universal consciousness, and in Saturn those weaknesses of appetites, those tendencies to use the power or position for gratifying its own ego—or self. These should be lost the more in that universal consciousness of the whole.

Then, it would be well if the entity itself would choose its own ide-als—spiritual, mental and material, and make application of same, first finding self.

As indicated from Mercury and Mars the entity is not only high-minded but capable of seeing the shady side of that wherein it may take advantage for self. These may materially apply for the moment, but thine own conscience would confuse thee.

In the fields of activity that have to do with the scientific reactions, as will be seen from the pattern in the earth, those that have to do with finance and personal as well as general properties, the entity may make the material as well as the mental and spiritual success—if there is the application of self in the specific or definite directions as may be pointed out from the individual or particular sojourns of the entity through the consciousness or awareness in Mercury, Mars, Jupiter, and even Saturn.

All of these, then, are but signposts along the way.

Then, first study self; knowing in whom as well as in what you be-lieve; not condemning any. For, with what measure you mete, it is mea-sured to you again. Inasmuch as you do it to the least of your brethren, you do it to thy Maker.

Thus there is instilled in each soul, as with this entity, the conscious-ness of its relationships to others, and those measures in which it may apply self not merely for gratifying but for giving the opportunities to others that have lost their way.

Thus, as a lecturer, as a teacher, as one applying mechanical as well as medicinal means to the own welfare as well as the welfare of those about the entity. These indicate the trend of thought of the individual . . .

Before that the entity was in the Egyptian land, among those that led the clannish peoples that were outpouring from the Uranian applica-tion, as well as in the application of treatments themselves.

Yet we find the entity being disturbed by these at times, bringing to the experience questionings as to the factors that control this or that experience.

This also gives the entity an interest in that which is new, or the application of old thoughts into new ideals, and not ideas alone.

The entity then was among the children of the Law of One, though those activities had been overrun by its own peoples, and the study of those things pertaining to the unfoldment from conception to the noon-day experience of life, and those that would deal with the application of self in the periods of unfoldment. These become problems in the entity's present experience. Where there are cause and effect in the spiritual attributes of the body, there are those influences of cause and effect in the life experience of those that apply themselves, either to the arts or in the cultivation of lands or in the studies of unusual natures. All bring their wonderment, and used in those directions may bring to the entity the greater experiences wherein it may study to show itself approved unto God, a workman not ashamed, yet rightly dividing the words of admonition, as well as the activities that are felt by the entity itself.

In the fields of service as a helper in administering to those afflicted in body, mind or soul, as well as to their physical needs—these are the works for the entity. For, these indicate the application of the tenets that may bring harmony to the experience.

Ready for questions.

(Q) *Any suggestions as to how I may place character analysis on a scientific basis before the medical profession?*

(A) As the entity in the Atlantean and Egyptian experience aided in preparing individuals for vocational activity, there are the tendencies to analyze conditions; remembering, in such, the spiritual, the mental, the material. While they are one, as an entity, in their manifestations in the earth they become as fields of service in which the development and unfoldment of the soul, or the undeveloped soul, may seek to find out-lets. Thus, as a psychoanalyst, as one keeping data we will find abilities by this entity.

(Q) *Would I be able to help more people by entering character or vocational analysis work, and leaving the practice of medicine?*

(A) In entering the character analysis and vocational guidance, the same *principles* must be applied. As to the tenets or the actual adminis-tering, these must be left out—if the greater experience would come to the entity.

Know in whom as well as in what you believe. Know as to who is the author of same, and consider that all things are possible with God. As within self, it is possible to become one whom many will call blessed. For, the very application of self in truths that pertain to the light—not as the light of the sun, but rather in that light of the *Son*. For He *is* the way, the truth and the life.

(Q) Then, you would advise continuing the practice of medicine?

(A) The use of those applications of psychoanalysis or vocational direction in preference to the medical application,

though use the same principles.

(Q) Give suggestions as to best way to go about this.

(A) First find self, and know thy ideal. Then make practical application. So live that ye never ask another to do that you would not do yourself, if conditions were reversed.

Reading 3175–1

Dream, yes—and hold to those counsels, those directions often found there, but keep thy head, keep thy feet.

Do not be misled by the confusion of an hour or of a circumstance. Know in whom, in what, ye believe. Know the author of thy faith. Know the author of thy confidences. Then apply those tenets that are truths in same.

For, there is a way that seemeth right, but the end is confusion. But in Him who is the light, there is no confusion. For He is the way, the truth, and the light; He has promised to meet thee in the temple of thine own body. And as given, "I knock—if ye will but open, I will enter in."

Reading 3132–1

Know within self what you believe. Know the author of your belief, spiritually as well as mentally and materially. Then be willing to live, to stand, to do those things you know to be your conviction as to the correct manner in which they should be done; guiding the same by the spirit of truth, the universality of man's dependency one upon another, to the glory of the Father in all things. For it is in Him we live and move and have our being.

And your purpose in the earth is, in every opportunity, in every activity one to or with another, to show forth His love until He comes again. For, remember ever, "In the manner as ye do it unto thy fellow man, ye do it unto thy Maker."

6

●

Be of Service

Reading 270-33

(Q) *Please guide me with information that will enable me to become of greater service to my fellow man.*

(A) There's none better than we have given, and as may be followed by that which may be brought to the awareness of self through the *practical* application of those meditative forces that come by setting aside a definite time, a period during each day's activity when there will be the purifying of the body, as in accord with that which would make for consecrating of self in all of its efforts, all of its abilities, and entering into the holy of holies within self for that talk with thy God within thyself. These efforts on the part of any soul will bring those things that make for the greater peace and happiness and the abilities to meet those emergencies of every nature that arise within the physical and mental bodies of a living body. For then the God forces that are the creative energies of the soul-mind will become the ruling forces in the life and in its activity in same; making for those abilities wherein any soul, any entity, may become the greater service, the greater factor in its associations with its fellow man. It is not how much one knows that counts, but how well one applies that it knows; in just being, doing, thinking, that which is pointed out to self through such constant, con-sistent, *practical* dependence upon the creative forces that have promised ever to meet one—everyone—when sought. And there will come that which is for the greater development in the soul forces of such an one that seeks.

Reading 270–46

(Q) Will you advise why I have not made greater progress in my service with the Western Union and what qualifications I lack that will enable me to be of greater service to the company and my associates?

(A) As indicated, the personal animosities of individuals. To be sure, this should not be—but personalities exist, and such conditions are a part of the experience of every individual. These should be met in ways and manners that are in keeping with that the individual sets as an ideal relationship between the employer and employee.

Reading 316–1

(Q) Is it best that a reconciliation be effected that will culminate in marriage?

(A) Provided that such reconciliation is in order or accord with the ideals of self, that have been builded in the experience, as to the relationship.

(Q) Is there something more than my own feelings and convictions that cause me to think that he still cares for me? or the fact that it is the desire of my heart for it to be so?

(A) It is a fact that, as we have given, there is the conviction in the heart of each that the better relationships for the good of each may come through their being joined together in their efforts in this present experience.

Yet, as given, to crucify self's ideals to the whims or fancies of any man is not development for the body!

(Q) Why do I feel responsible for the whole affair, and responsible for the future?

(A) Because there has been a great deal of resentment builded by implication, by the body—or the man. Hence there are those periods when, with the thinking or meditating over the past, the resentment is turned towards self!

Do not condemn self! Rather make self's life one of service to an ideal, and leave the whole in the hands of the Creative Forces that rule the destinies of every soul!

Make self more and more in accord with that which is of His ways—
the *Master's* ways, and leave the results in His hands.

For, in Him—in *Him*—we live and move and have our being!

Reading 410–2

In entering the present experience, much might be said respecting
the soul's purpose in the present experience, and the determinations
that may be said to have been set. And while there have been those
periods in the experience of the entity when there apparently were all
those things necessary that would—and could—make for that which
would be the impulse to carryon, in this experience, to the fulfilling of
all those desires, some of these in the first of this association being
denied—as it were—then, as from the forces outside of self, apparently
so little at first was left for that to which the entity and soul had builded.
Yet these things, these experiences, rather than making for misunder-
standings, should make the entity rather know that those joys, those
things in the desires, may be better prepared even by separations. For,
where the heart is, there will the mind be enjoined. For, the treasures of
the heart are the sincere desires to be used as a channel that will be the
greater manifestation of that which is set as the ideal in the mental and
the spiritual self. *Know*, then, He doeth all things well.

Reading 452–7

As given, there must—or there would, from the developments from
the soul forces of the entity—come those periods when there would be
within self halting opinions, and questionings within self, and
questionings of others and their purposes, aims, desires. While, as given,
tolerance in all directions is a thing to be desired, much greater indeed
is to know the love that is given by Him who gave Himself as a sacrifice,
as an example, as a mediator, as an influence in the experience of every
soul. To know, then, the consciousness within self of the indwelling of
the spirit of the love of the Master raiseth each soul to the knowledge to
do that which is to the soul the necessary activity for *that* soul to develop. For, the gospel of Jesus Christ taketh man where man is, for the
making aware is of the soul's relation to the spirit that gives life in every
man.

Hence in these meditations, in these activities, there may come that which will enable this body–soul, this body–mind, to become active in that field whereunto there will be not only peace and joy and happiness in this present experience, but there will be builded soul development in the entity's activities itself.

Be willing, then, to give *out*. Not only of self's own ideas, but of self's own ideals; and *dare* to live that as the conscience directs thee, but be—most of all—sincere with self, with self's own soul, with self's own ideal. For, the ideal is set in Him, and must *not* be shaken.

Reading 949-2

Where there are ideals builded and adhered to, and these placed within those realms of the Creative Forces—that deal with man's experience in the earth, and man's relationship one to another, that make for those developments through the continuity of life's *force* flowing through same—may the entity gain in the present. Either in giving those that come through song or music, that may awaken much in the experience of others—but also serving in a manner that keeps self's *own* ideal first and foremost for self, without inducing or forcing another to see a like vision. Keep self aright. Be true to self and thou will not be false to any man. Remember, the Creative Forces make for a continual development in material and spiritual forces.

Reading 1742-2

(Q) *What can I do to use my unfoldment for others?*
(A) Give out; even as ye have received, give unto others.

(Q) *Do I still need to unfold in an individual way before helping others in any definite way?*
(A) In helping, in giving out to others may the unfoldment come; not in those things that would become as *evil-spoken* of, but in little acts of kindness, little words here and there for little by little, line upon line, precept upon precept, does one gain in self, and add to others.

Reading 1786-2

As we find, as has been given, the entity needs to study that which has been outlined for the entity and to go about making practical application of same in its *daily* relation, ships to others.

Not that any information would be given that would enable the entity to just pick up self and transplant to this or that place. It must be an inward development!

As has been outlined, first study self. What *do* you desire? Is it selfish, is it only for self; is it only that there may be the gratifying of an emotion, an appetite, a physical desire? Or is there not something that is more lasting, something that is desired to be of a *helpful* force for someone else?

Is there really the desire to know love, or to know the experience of someone having an emotion over self? Is it a desire to be itself expended in doing that which may be helpful or constructive? This *can* be done, but it will require the *losing* of self, as has been indicated, *in* service for others. . .

(Q) *Should I continue through life alone?*

(A) If this seems well—or does this seem well? or is [it] the self that you are looking for! Do something for someone else! Make their lives happy, make their lives worthwhile, and then there may be those experiences that will come! But arise to that consciousness that if ye would have life, if ye would have friends, if ye would have love, these things ye must expend. For only that ye give away do ye possess.

Reading 1800–28
[Background: Reading given for Home Health Remedies Corp., requested by Hugh Lynn Cayce]

You are working under conditions that to you are not satisfactory, but if you are not giving your best under these conditions, if you had the *ideal* conditions you wouldn't give your best either! and don't fool yourself that you would! Because he that says he would give to the poor if he had a million, and doesn't give when he has ten cents, wouldn't give if he had a million! The same applies in the preparations of those things that represent ideals and principles and purposes. Not that ye are perfect but that ye would *grow!*

Reading 1877–1

The entity has the inclination, owing to the exercising of the influences as indicated, to become too easily dependent upon others.

Rather learn the lesson as He has given, that he that would be the greatest among you, among his brethren, among his fellow men, will serve *them* the more—rather than depending upon them. And know that His strength, if ye will abide in Him, will sustain thee always, and will bear thee up, in those periods of disturbance or distress.

For know, as He gave, so long as ye are in the material experience, of the awareness of fleshly desires, it must indeed be that offenses come. Just let *none* be offended in thy neglect, in thy willful carelessness, in thy desire for power or for position.

But rather give place to humbleness, that ye may shine the greater for thy Lord, for thy God.

Who, then, *is* thy ideal? And in such *live*—not put it up to be looked at alone, but live towards others as ye would have others live towards thee. Counsel others in those fields of service, those fields of activity in which ye would have others guide thee.

For in the surrounding of self with His presence, there comes the ability to counsel with any, in any phase of man's experience in the material sojourns.

From the Uranian influence we find the interest in the mystic or occult forces as a part of man's experience. For as the mind has given and does give power to all those influences of which it has been a part, so is the power wielded.

For as He has indicated, that ye think in thy heart, that ye become; just as that alone which ye assimilate in thy body becomes a part of thy life-blood.

So, in thy spiritual and mental life, keep in those ways that will bring the more and more consciousness that He stands not at thy door but that He walks and He talks with thee! and thy garden of love and light is filled with His presence; and ye show these in the manner of thy thought, thy conversation, thy dealings with thy fellow man.

As to the appearances in the earth, and the activities that these produce as impelling forces and influences in the present experience—we find that these, as has been indicated, have been mitigated or changed much by the application of self as to the laws, the rules, the regulations of individual activity in relationship to Creative Forces.

Then, what is Creative Force—an influence in the affairs of an individual, as thyself?

Good, as it comes in any form, is creative, is constructive; and thus, as one applies same—without the thought of self, but that others may know peace and harmony in their experience—it brings such an awakening as ye have experienced oft as ye sought to feel the vibrations through thy body, or to feel and hear and know, through the lights of thy consciousness upon the affairs and thoughts of others—bringing the exhilarating feeling of nearness to that Creative Energy.

Reading 1957–1

(Q) With what firm or organization is it best for me to work?

(A) That must be determined within self, according to what is the ideal. Then, with any organization, know what are their policies. If they are in keeping with those things which have been indicated that should be thy purpose, then with such an organization connect thyself.

(Q) Is there any connection of value to me by considering the work of [1849] . . . N.Y.C.?

(A) This depends upon just what phase the entity would select as a field or an outlet for its activity. Worth considering, sure—for it offers a field of service—but *give—give—give,* if you would have!

(Q) What opportunities would the business of H.R—N.Y. offer me?

(A) Again, the entity is to choose as to policies, as to purposes, as to ideals. Are they in keeping with thine own, do they answer to thine own, can you work with and use those policies and hold to thine own? Well, you would hardly think so! but these should be considered as to thine *own* self! For the field is to be chosen not for the money alone, but remember thy ideal—body, mind and soul! As has been indicated, do not be afraid of giving self in a service—if the *ideal* is correct. If it is for selfish motives, for aggrandizement, for obtaining a hold to be used in an underhand manner, *beware.* If it is that the glory of truth may be made manifest, *spend it all*—whether self, mind, body, or the worldly means—whether in labor or in the coin of the realm.

Reading 1998–1

First, know thy ideal—spiritually, mentally, materially. Not so much as to what you would like others to be, but what may be *your* ideal relationships to others! For he that is the greatest is the servant of all—as the law of cause and effect. That in some instances of least resistance is the influence most needed. In others, that most positive in being the better conductor of force and power is the influence needed.

Reading 2030-1

Then, your ideal is not what you may acquire by "Gimmie—Gimmie—Gimmie," but "What may I do, what may I give, in my relationships to others to make that association the *beautiful experience*," for which ye long so always!

Then the ideal is, "What may I do or be to others, that they may be better, may have a greater concept of the purposes of life, by even being acquainted or associated with myself?"

This should be your ideal, in your material life.

It is not that the body is all of meat, nor all of position, nor all of that activity in a social manner, nor all of play or work—but *all* of these enter into the experience. Just as the mental and spiritual body apply, or need, or rely upon the attributes of the phases of the whole, so is it necessary that there be the ideal in the material relationships. And these also must, as in mind, have a spiritual conception—if you would grow in grace, in knowledge, in understanding.

Then, as you find: If you would have friends, show yourself to be a friend to others. If you would have love in your life, it is necessary that you be *lovely* to others. If you would have that in your material experience to supply the physical needs of the body, the gratifying or satisfying or contenting of self in its relationships to material things, *work* in such a manner that others may be *inspired* by that manner in which you conduct yourself.

Not as one afraid—neither as one that is unmindful of the body needs or the body privileges. But abuse *not* your opportunities, if you would be the gainer in this experience.

Reading 2056-2

(Q) Regarding his connection with . . . in view of that which seems to be afoot, what should this body do relative to his association with this company?

(A) Discontinue connection with any condition that to the body-consciousness is not in keeping with the best development of self, or of others. Never well to do evil or any underhanded thing that individuals or groups may benefit materially from same. Rather live that life that *merits* the best through *service* given to others—for the laborer is ever worthy of hire, and the Lord hath given and hath established that, "He that walketh in the way of the just shall receive the fat of the land." Let the Lord be thy God, rather than position, power, or fame—for in service to Him may the heart find that satisfaction that comes with a life being *well* spent, and do not so act that self-condemnation enters into thine inmost self.

(Q) *Give the body any other advice that would be in keeping for the best development for this body.*

(A) Keep thine face toward the light, and the shadows will not bring fright—for fear is the beginning of all undoing. Keep the heart singing, and the Lord will raise thee up to *magnify* His promises to men through service to thine fellow man, for he that lends to the Lord lays up a store in that realm where thieves do not break through nor steal. Keep thine ways open, above censure, and *never* censure self.

Reading 2901–1

As to the application, then, of the truths, in the experiences of the entity in the earth's plane, as is seen, there will come the opportunity for the entity to gain and to rule, and to use earthly goods. Then apply those things that are in hand towards the service of the Creator, for in service to man is the highest service to the Maker, for man is that portion of the Maker which may be *physically* served. Then keep the way straight, walking in that way that leads to closer communion with the Giver of life and light.

Reading 2959–1

Do keep that mental attitude of being not only good but good for something. Have a definite goal as a contribution not only to the pleasure of self but for someone else, or for several others, sometime each day. Think of others, for in the helping of others you will help yourself.

Reading 2954–1

As to the abilities of the entity in the present, that to which it may attain, and how:

As given, first know thyself, thy ideals, thy mental attributes, thy physical weakness and thy physical strength. Do not fail to become acquainted with these.

In those activities of service where there is a greater respect of those about self are the greater opportunities, though they may be in the opposite sex—for they, too, may be endowed with the spirit of helpfulness from above, even as thou mayest be.

But keep the umbrella of fate over the entity, and ye will find ye may walk in the way that is pleasing to Him.

Turning those abilities into channels of self-indulgence, self-aggrandizement, we may bring quite questionable influences into the experience.

But keeping the faith will keep greater confidence in self, as well as manifestedly in others.

Reading 3005–1

(Q) How can I change my mode of living to be stronger and more helpful to my family?

(A) As the disorder and disturbance has caused the greater part of the changes in the present, we find that as conditions improve, and as the opportunities are given, the body may apply self in those directions that are given from time to time.

For, each entity should be a channel of blessing and of helpfulness to others.

Little has been given here as to the attitude, for this special reason; for the body in itself as to its mental attitude is well. For, to be of help to others is the ideal of the entity. Keep that. Never as of a self glory, but to the glory of the Son in the Father, and to the honor of self.

Reading 3034–2

(Q) What day and month and year would be the best to open my office and practice in California?

(A) That depends very much upon many other conditions. For the duration, if begun here, you will keep it. And then a time after that when there has been the completing of the post–graduate courses, begin the service to others. But in the application of self, do not attempt to live upon but live for others. If you live upon others, you will be a failure. If you live for others, you may be a success.

(Q) *Any other advice?*

(A) As indicated, get the ideal! He that would be the greatest success will be the servant of all, and not the boss or the commander but working with and for others.

Reading 3059–1

The mental attitude should be creative; not merely ideals that are passive, but ideals that are active in the relationships of the body to those it meets. The associations, to this entity, mean a great deal.

Do not bore others, but if you have something to give in spiritual instruction without hampering others, give it; or, as He who is the way and the life, give—for He gave continuously that needed. Give thou continuously that which meets the needs, that answers for the faith that lies within; thinking of others as well as of self. For with the same measure ye mete to thy fellow man ye are giving just that measure of service to thy Maker.

Reading 3575–2

As to the abilities of the entity in the present, that to which it may attain and how: Keep peace within thine own heart, not to the exclusion of that prompted by thy conscience, but know that the Lord liveth and that He requireth of thee the using wisely of that lent thee, even as indicated in the parable of the talents. For many are in thine hands and the Lord loveth the cheerful giver, not merely of self, not merely to others. Help others to help themselves, rather than giving that which makes them poor indeed.

Reading 3659–1

(Q) *How can I develop a more pleasant personality?*

(A) We have indicated as to how there should be the application of self, not to the curious, but towards being a means of help to someone else. And let the joy of this alone bring its own reward in peace and harmony, and in a pleasing personality. But make the individuality true, and the personality will shine through the individuality.

Reading 3478–2

We find in Venus the appreciation of home, and yet never giving much thought or care—as the entity would imply in self, or really innately feels that self has a good excuse—but don't use it as an excuse! Rather let it be as thy purpose to contribute to the welfare of others. But do in self first practice spirituality. This doesn't imply that the entity is not high-minded, for we have just given that it is—but practice! You will be able in ministering physically or mentally to give others much greater and more far-reaching influences, as well as self, by giving individuals something to live for, within as well as without themselves! For he that contributes only to his own welfare soon finds little to work for. He that contributes only to the welfare of others soon finds too much of others and has lost the appreciation of self, or of its ideals.

Reading 3665–1

First analyze self in relationships to the entity's ideals; not merely as an oral analysis within self, but as to the ideals that may have grown to seed, the ideals of the entity that may expect God's blessings on everyone and thus are creative in their essence and in their activity. These should be the manners of analyzing.

Then when these ideals have been found, apply them in thy work physically, as well as in maintaining order, peace, confidence in those groups of various faiths, of various abilities, throughout the entity's activities.

Reading 288–4

(Q) Is the body following its proper vocation?

(A) It is, for in this is the spirit and soul (through the mental forces and the physical) are being awakened through these forces as exercised in the present mental forces, is reaching out to that development necessary for this entity to give of its best self to others. As in this: We should (all the human family) recognize this fact. Man, or woman, cannot give toward the Creator; and those kindnesses, those unselfish forces, those givings of self to His creatures are lending to the Lord.

Reading 3752-1

(Q) What suggestions have you to make that would add to entity's peace of mind?

(A) That is as has just been given. Find that the ideal is unattainable, that to be sure—this the body has lost hold of, as respecting its spiritual life. The necessity of constant attaining and attaining without the use of same in bringing that same vision of the ideal as held by self into the lives, the minds, of others, is that to which the entity should give *much* of self. Not as one that would seek to gain for self, and *gain* in same, save as in the use of the abilities *in* self to make life more worthwhile for the *other* fellow; for one may only gain the vision of the promises within self and self's relation to the Creative Forces, by assisting the other fellow. Not that the God of the Fathers, or of man, needs any aid of any man at any time, but lending to the Lord *is* gained through aid to the other fellow.

7

●

Setting and Living by Ideals

Reading 24–4

Oft may it be asked, *what is* an ideal? That not made with hands; that that is *eternal—that* is an ideal. Keep self in accord, in attune with those forces as may make manifest through self in mental and spiritual manners—and this will keep one in attune with an ideal as may be set before self. Being true first to self, will prevent self from being false to anyone. Be not too close mouthed in expression of thoughts, for in the *use* of that as is held *or* known, or had in hand, is development obtained. Know in whom thou hast believed, knowing He is able to keep that which is committed unto thee against any experience. Keep *self* unspotted, but be not sulky in doing so!

Reading 256–2

An ideal means that to which the entity may, itself, ever look up, knowing itself to be gradually becoming a portion, but *never* may it be the whole. Something to look up to, or to attempt to *attain* to; not an idea, that I may do this or I may do that, that I may accomplish such and such through such modes of operation! for then one reaches the goal! An ideal is that as is sought by, and developed to be, at an at-onement with same, a portion of same, but never the whole.

Reading 270–31

(Q) Will you give further enlightenment to help accomplish this desire?

(A) The basis of every entity's activity should be the placing of an ideal in the experiences of self. Not an idol, not an idea, not a position even that may be attained in the earth's experience by earthly activities; for to attain that which is wholly desired in the mental abilities of an entity is to become stale and self-centered. Then, naturally, the retrogression would ensue.

Hence, the attaining of that which makes for the better and greater development in the earth's experience is to be wholly *dependent*, in the mental-spiritual activities, upon the will of the Creator, or Creative Forces, that may manifest through every activity of self; making self then a channel day by day in the direction that is set as the ideal of the *soul*, not of the mental mind.

This does not mean that an entity becomes impractical, or unpractical, or unethical, nor long-faced, nor sober, nor indulging in criticism of those that do not think or act as self. Rather, it is seeing in the individual whom an entity or body hates (or dislikes, because of activities) that which such an entity or body would worship as God!

For, each activity is a manifestation of the forces that emanate from the universal, or the consciousness of the living God! Individuals' activity upon that, by their construction of same, makes it hell or heaven!

Then, each soul should see more and more constructively in regard to the most destructive influences in an activity!

One that does not accomplish this loses, or besets self to self's own undoing!

For, even as He, though He were the Son, He thought it not robbery to be equal with God, yet made Himself of no estate that He might fulfill the law and show the way; and, though suffering in body, in mind, being despised, spit upon, hated, He gave, "Father, forgive them, they know not what they do."

This should be the *impelling* attitude of everyone that seeks to abide in the presence of the Creator.

Reading 282–6

(Q) What are the highest ideals that should be followed by the body-mind in all his business activities?

(A) "As ye would that men should do to you, do ye even so to them." Loving God, in body, mind and soul; keeping self unspotted from the world; eschewing evil; loving thy neighbor, thy brother, as thyself. This is the whole law. This is the ideal that He, the Master, gave. And when one walks, talks, thinks, acts in such a way and manner, He is faithful in that He gave, "I will not leave thee comfortless but my presence, my consciousness, will abide with thee, giving thee the thought, the word, that thou shouldst think at all times." Trust ye in Him.

Reading 357-13

The mind uses its spiritual ideals to build upon. And the mind also uses the material desires as the destructive channels, or it is the interference by the material desires that prevents a body and a mind from keeping in perfect accord with its ideal.

Thus, these continue ever in the material plane to be as warriors one with another. Physical emergencies or physical conditions may oft be used as excuses, or as justifications for the body choosing to do this or that. Ought these things so to be, according to thy ideal?

Then, the more important, the most important experience of this or any individual entity is to first know what *is* the ideal—spiritually.

Who and what is thy pattern?

Throughout the experience of man in the material world, at various seasons and periods, teachers or "would-be" teachers have come; setting up certain forms or certain theories as to manners in which an individual shall control the appetites of the body or of the mind, so as to attain to some particular phase of development.

There has also come a Teacher who was bold enough to declare Himself as the Son of the living God. He set no rules of appetite. He set no rules of ethics, other than "As ye would that men should do to you, do ye even so to them," and to know "Inasmuch as ye do it unto the least of these, thy brethren, ye do it unto thy Maker." He declared that the kingdom of heaven is within each individual entity's consciousness, to be attained, to be aware of—through meditating upon the fact that God is the Father of every soul.

Jesus, the Christ, is the mediator. And in Him, and in the study of His examples in the earth, is *life—and* that ye may have it more abundantly.

He came to demonstrate, to manifest, to give life and light to all.

Here, then, ye find a friend, a brother, a companion. As He gave, "I call ye not servants, but brethren." For, as many as believe, to them He gives power to become the children of God, the Father; joint heirs with this Jesus, the Christ, in the knowledge and in the awareness of this presence abiding ever with those who set this ideal before them.

What, then, is this as an ideal?

As concerning thy fellow man, He gave, "As ye would that others do to you, do ye even so to them." Take no thought, worry not, be not overanxious about the body. For He knoweth what ye have need of. In the place thou art, in the consciousness in which ye find yourself, is that which is *today, now*, needed for thy greater, thy better, thy more wonderful unfoldment. But today *hear* His voice, "Come unto me, all that are weak or that are heavy-laden, and I will give you rest from those worries, peace from those anxieties." For the Lord loveth those who put their trust *wholly* in Him.

This, then, is that attitude of mind that puts away hates, malice, anxiety, jealousy. And it creates in their stead, in that mind is the builder, the fruits of the spirit—love, patience, mercy, long-suffering, kindness, gentleness. And these—against such there is no law. They break down barriers, they bring peace and harmony, they bring the outlook upon life of not finding fault because someone "forgot," someone's judgment was bad, someone was selfish today. These ye can overlook, for so did He. In His own experience with those that He had chosen out of the world, if He had held disappointment in their leaving Him to the mercies of an indignant high priest, a determined lawyer and an unjust steward, what would have been *thy* hope, thy promise today?

Reading 987–4

Then ask thyself the question—gain the answer first in thy physical consciousness:

"What is my ideal of a *spiritual* life?"

Then when the answer has come—for it has been given by Him that is Life—that the kingdom of God, the kingdom of heaven, is within; and we view the kingdom of God without by the application of those things that are of the spirit of truth—These then answered, ye seek again in the inner consciousness: "Am I true to my ideal?"

These become then the answers. This and that and the other; never as pro and con. For the growth in the spirit is as He has given; ye *grow* in grace, in knowledge, in understanding.

Reading 1082–3

These interpretations that are given from the activities as seen here are that: The ideal is not as a material thing, not as only a mental experience, but as the mental, the material and the spiritual world.

For life *is* the manifestation of that Divine which is worshiped as God.

Hence each soul–entity is a portion of same, with that privilege through the experiences in materiality to manifest an ideal and thus grow in grace, in knowledge, in faith, in hope, in love; that the entity, the soul, may be one with the Creative Forces—that should be the ideal of every soul.

Reading 1755–3

First, know what is thy own ideal. Not as to what others may do for thee, but what is the ideal way of individuals to live among themselves? What believest thou as to those things pertaining to the relationship of self, as an individual, to the Creative Forces or God? What manner of expression should self give as in its relationships to same? Not more of freedom of speech or of activity than you would desire of self, would you impose or express upon others.

In whom hast thou believed? What is the source of thy faith, of thy hope? And then—so live, so act among others, that ye are a living example of that ye believe.

Reading 3481–2

We would, then, rather give the entity the ideal manner in which the abilities may be applied, and thus the entity must choose for itself.

Know that ye are in a material world. True, ye are body, mind and spirit, but do not expect spiritual things to happen in material manifestations save as a helpful experience if used so, for the entity producing that which may be as a helpful, encouraging experience, and don't look for those things to materialize save by necessity. For did the Master even feed the disciples when in the normal manner there could be food purchased? Did He draw from the fish monies to buy clothing, to buy trips, to buy experiences for Himself or [His] disciples? or to meet emergencies?

Ye, as most individuals, and ye in a little manner, observe these and yet would have others believe differently. In the application, then, first know what ye believe, spiritually, and who is the author of thy ideal. Remember there are not authors, it is not plural. For the Lord, thy God, is one. Don't forget it! He's not multiple; there are helpers, yes, but each individual soul is meant to help.

Are ye doing your job or trusting someone else to do it for thee? It can't be done! Each soul is just as each atom, as each corpuscle. For, remember, ye are as corpuscles in the body of God. Each with a duty, a function to perform if the world would be better for thou having lived in it, and this is thy purpose in the earth.

Know, then, in whom ye believe and in what ye believe, spiritually; then know what is thy idea and also thy ideal mentally. For mind is the builder. For it partakes both of materiality and eternity and spirituality. These know, for these are true. The results in thy experience materially should be, will be when ye are assured, pleasing first in the sight of God and harmonious in thine own experience.

Reading 4866–2

(Q) *In reference to answer #3 in first reading, what is it that this body would worship?*

(A) That is as to what this body will make as its ideal; fame, position, politically, financially, or that which is a well-balanced life, knowing those attributes are necessary that have been given or shown for the better development, that will bring in the mental and material life a contentment, a satisfaction; yet not wholly ever satisfying, for when one becomes satisfied they begin to deteriorate. *Contentment* makes for that which may be sought by all, that which brings the most happiness, the most hope, the most optimistic outlook upon all activities of the body. *This—as* to what the body would worship—must be set, as to what is the body's ideal.

(Q) What is the body's ideal?

(A) *That* the body must set itself; for this is as the *will* of the body. The body *knows* within self that which it holds as the criterion for *every* developing life, from that *it* holds as its ideal. Then, *whatever* is set in self the body should work toward, and the results will be in keeping with that activity. As given, should the body set the ideal wholly in making the material success, it may *not* expect to be content, nor will it bring happiness. If the body's ideal is set in that which is *right* in the sight of its ideal, or by the measurement of that it holds as its criterion, as its ideal, *that* it will develop to. That must be set by self. What does the body set as its *spiritual* ideal, as its moral ideal, as its ideal in social, political or economic conditions? Are they in keeping with that one who is the Giver of all good and perfect gifts, or are they creative in themselves? This the body must answer for self.

Ideals and Ideas

Reading 165–24

What is the first thing? *Self!* and the willingness to give self; willingness to suffer in self in ideas, in the physical surroundings, for an *ideal!* Not merely idealistic but an ideal that requires first *courage*; the dare to do the impossible. For with God nothing is impossible, and the individual that may give himself as a channel through which the influences of good may come to others may indeed be guided or shown the way. For the influences of such a nature are those that all men seek, and for which there is a great cry in the earth today—and *today is* the accepted time!

Reading 172–3

One that loves music, and the art of music; as a critic, rather than as applied. As the voice of individuals or of nature, rather than as instrumental, so far as any individual instrument concerned. Rather in groups and masses arid their altering in harmony and its changes, for at times harmony is desired by the entity. Then contrasts are necessary for the entity to *understand* conditions that, to the entity, comparisons may be drawn. Hence innately in *every* element, whether in affairs of the heart, of life, of position, of stations in life, there is ever the comparison drawn by the entity. Well, then, that the entity *attain* for self an ideal, rather than mere ideas. Drawing often upon the innate influences in self as related to the mysteries of life, as pertaining to the mysteries of the beyond—in which the entity often delves, that there may be for the self the greater fullness of the experiences of the entity. To experience, to the entity, is to understand.

Reading 257–181

(Q) Is [257] in a position now with the above situations pending to be assured of coming out of the depression and out of debt and again being re-established?

(A) Provided the ideal—and not merely an idea—is carried forward; and that the ideal is not drenched in self-indulgence, aggrandizement or glory by any of the associates and of [257] himself. Boast not thyself of yesterday nor today, unless thy conscience be clear with him who may have been to thine own mind thy worst enemy. For that ye worship as thy God is God of thine enemy also!

Reading 279–15

(Q) Am I right in taking sides with [2107] and associates, in their attitude and actions regarding Pittsburgh Chemical?

(A) That, again, must be the opinion—or decided by self, rather than that as may be given; for each entity is a universe within its own self, with its ideals and ideas that have been builded within self as to what the proper associations and relations with individuals *should* be, and when there are differences of opinions, or activities of individuals *or* groups *with* whom a body may associate or affiliate themselves, then that as is the criterion of a body's ideal must enter in and make for them those decisions in which, or through which, their lots *must* be cast. That which may aid may only be as was long ago given to that one *called* Lot. As to whether you shall separate yourself from this *or* that are the *decisions* that are given to each entity as a *will*, and each acts upon same with the proper consideration of *all* things that go to make up differences in a group, or an individual's activities towards associations of any agent, or of any officer of whatever group or corporation one may affiliate their activities with.

Reading 1739–6

If that towards ideas are in keeping with the *ideals*, follow those. Have *ideals*, not *ideas!* Ideas may be as thoughts, made criminal or miracles. Be sure the *ideal* is proper. Follow that irrespective of outside influence. Know self is right, and then go straight ahead. So live each and every day that you may look any man in the face and tell him to go to hell!

Reading 2716–1

One close to the cusps or changes in the zodiacal signs. Thus one who has periods of quite confusing influences within self; temperamental, as it may be termed, and yet it is the result of confusion within self. There is the desire that others give an expression of opinion, yet there is innately reserved in the entity the forming of its own conclusions, even from the opinions of others. This is very well, if the ideals of the entity are ideals and not ideas alone. Ideals have their basic principle in spiritual import. While the mind is the builder, that as bespeaks of self or selfishness is ideas, not ideals.

Reading 2798–1

Thus may the entity find in its present experience those same laws of cause and effect, of give and take, of that cycle in which that ye prepare yourself for—through mind, through body—ye may build into thy experience. Thus sacrifices of self, yes; of self's ideas, yes; of self's ideals, no. For there is One, even Him—who is the way, the truth and the light. And He blessed children, as ye may also—in thy ministry to them. For in them is ever the hope of the world. Here, then, ye have the opportunity of so using, so applying thyself as to build bodies that are indeed temples of the living God; also minds that may be wholly acceptable unto Him. In this ye may aid the bringing of that day of the Lord to hand.

Reading 3211–2

One definitely given to those things pertaining to a universal consciousness. Thus in any direction in which the entity may choose to be argumentative or active, the entity will find the ability at least materially, mentally or spiritually, to justify that stand taken. These may not all be cooperative or coordinated. The entity must learn indeed to understand that pronouncement, "Know, 0 Israel, the Lord thy God is one Lord." These, then, are body, mind, soul. Spirit, mentality, physical conditions—these are all a part one of the other. They grow or deteriorate according to the manner in which those activities or ideas or mental concepts or precepts are coordinate. For as given, body, and mind and soul are the finite expressions of Father, Son and Holy Spirit; time, space and patience. All of these are one when they are coordinative in their activity. When they are not they are as opposing influences. These, men use as ideas; never as ideals but ideas. [Ideals] and [ideas] are quite different. One arises from the infinite, the other from the finite.

Reading 5502–2

For an idea and an ideal are two different things—an ideal is that that may be sought for, while an idea may lead into troubled waters.

Reading 1863–1

Not that it should be overly forward, but there are ideas and there are ideals. Ideals are of a spiritual nature that rest upon the general purposes of spiritual activity—that is, the seed sown will bring its fruit in due season. This in its full analysis is to be the basis of the activities.

Reading 3245–1

Changes will be indicated through Saturn, through Mercury the high mental abilities of the entity, through Jupiter the whole purpose of benevolence—always for the fellow that's in the minority, even if the minority is wrong. Watch this, being sure that there is not too enthusiastic reception of any idea without considering its necessity of being ideal; not idealistic, but ideal—or a pattern, and a pattern which ye may not only live by but die by and for.

Reading 5255–1

There are many commendable activities; there are also questionable ones. While the entity is very secure in itself, that is, as to its ideas, a question might be asked: Are the ideals true, are the activities in their relationships to others in keeping wholly with that which may be claimed as an ideal?

Have ye analyzed the difference between ideas and ideals? Ideals are set from spiritual purposes, spiritual aspirations, spiritual desires and there is a pattern in Him who is the way, the truth and the light, and when that pattern is set according to such judgments, we would find there is never condemning of another. Because others do not agree with thee, condemn them not. For with what judgment ye mete, it is measured to thee again. These ye find as thy greater problems in the present in relationships with others. Then analyze first thyself and thy ideals. Not merely as to, "Yes, I believe this," or "Yes, I believe that," but write it down.

What is thy spiritual ideal? Who is the author of same? Do ye apply same mentally? Is that what ye think of people?

Writing Ideals

Reading 830-3

Expend the self in study, in meditation; not by force but by the *opening* of self to recognize that as goes on about self. In this manner: Each day before retiring, make a resume—not just mentally but upon paper—of what have been the *experiences* of the whole day. Make this not only a rule but a rule to do; not to be studied, not to be exploited or shown or given to others, but for self! And *do not* read same after it is written for at least thirty days. And then note the difference in what you are thinking and what you are thinking about, what your desires are, what your experiences are!

And remember, do not condemn others, do not condemn self. But express desires, express wishes, express the kindnesses *you* have shown as well as the kindness others have shown. For know that the fruits of the spirit bring to an altering and a changing body the fruits of the spirit in measures that find expressions in the relationships to individuals. Do not attempt to be good but rather good *for something!* Know what is thy purpose, what is thy goal! And unless these are founded in constructive, spiritual construction, they will turn again upon thyself! For each soul is meeting day by day *self!*

Reading 1995-1

(Q) *In regard to my spiritual life, what do I need to feed my nature, and how may I get it?*

(A) Analyze self and the purposes, the motives, the influences; and know that they agree with that which is thy ideal.

What is thy ideal? spiritually, mentally, physically?

Not what you would wish God to do for you, but what may you do in appreciation of the love shown? Not as to what ye would like to be, but what may ye mentally give that will be conducive to constructive thinking in the experience of others?

In the physical, not what you want others to do for you, but what may you do for them? These are what we mean by constructive thinking, and as they are applied within the experience we will come to see what a spiritual life means. Not the eliminating of pleasures, for the purpose of life *is* pleasure, but that which is constructive and not destructive!

Reading 2021–1

One of the influences that must first be builded, then, is to first know thy ideals—spiritually, mentally, materially. And in the spiritual, know that the ideal must be that which is able to keep whatever may be committed unto it against *any* experience. In the mental, it must be ever constructive, creative in its influence, in its activity. In the material, it must be not what you would want others to do for you, but the ideal manner and way in which ye must meet those influences, those associations, those affiliations with thy fellow man. For, inasmuch, and in the manner as ye do unto the least of thy brethren, ye do unto thy Maker.

These as we find should be studied, analyzed, thought through; and, no matter *what* the cost may be, they should be lived up to, in accordance with that ideal.

And we will find that it will bring harmony, contentment, and sufficient of *every* worldly, spiritual, material thing necessary for thy soul development.

Then, what thy destiny is depends upon what ye will do with thyself in relationship to thy ideal.

Reading 2524–5

Then the beginning—for physical help as well as for the interpretations of self—is to begin with thy ideals. Set it down in black and white. Take yourself in hand and draw a picture. You're a pretty good engineer to draw pictures of other things. Did you ever try a picture of yourself? How far do you span from what you would be, or from what you would have others to think you are? How far does this stretch?

This should be begun, then, with the spirituality. What is thy ideal, spiritually? Who do you hope to see, where do you hope to go, when you leave here? Remember, He that gave the world compared man's life to a tree, in that where it falls that is where it stands. The life goes on, only the body remains. It returns to that which it has builded itself. Just as the rich man and Lazarus. Because of his patience, fortitude and brotherly love, Lazarus went to the bosom of faith, or in faith. Yet it was not apart from torment, though divided so very distinctly as to make a barrier that could never be crossed—in that realm of consciousness.

What is thy ideal mentally? Know that in the material plane, mind is the builder. Are thy ideals and thy conversations with thy associates consistent? They should be. For as the Master gave, "Consistency, thou art a jewel."

These, then, are the beginnings in the finding of self. And in the finding of self you will come closer to accomplishing that which may bring material as well as mental satisfaction in thy activities in the earth.

Do that, then, and you will come to know thyself better, and thy relationships with others will be more satisfactory, and there will no longer be the discontent within self or with self. For, if ye will have people interested in thee, interest thyself in people—and not by force. Ye like associations, ye like such activities. Why not practice it in thy life?

Reading 3032-2

Thus, as the injunction would be—from astrological as well as material sojourns—*study self.* Make not merely a mental analysis of self but write it:

What are thy spiritual ideals?

Where is heaven (to the entity)?

Where is God?

What relationship does the entity bear to the Creative Force? (And then underline what you are doing about it!)

What is religion?

What is morality?

What is patience?

Write these—as related to self, not to others.

Then thy mental ideal—how do ye attain to a consciousness? By merely saying and resaying, or by living and applying it in relationships to others?

What is the ideal mental ability? Ye have it as near as one in every million! In the material ideal, is it the satisfying of some material self, some appetite, some desire of body? or is it the fulfilling of a spiritual and mental purpose?

Write these, and then—as ye analyze self and apply, lay this aside—and then in three months check on self. It will be worthwhile.

Reading 3051–2

No soul enters by chance, but that it may fill that it has sought and does seek as its ideal. Hence, as may be the first injunction to this entity: Do not too oft accept what others say, *unless* it answers to a something deep within self.

Do not, then, merely have a verbal or vocal ideal. Do write what is thy ideal. Begin with that under these three headings: Spiritual, Mental, Material. And write what is thine own ideal. As ye may find, these may change from time to time. For, each soul grows in grace, in knowledge, in understanding. Just as the awareness, the unfoldments come to the self *as* the entity applies that it has chosen and does choose from day to day. And ye will find, this will enable thee to find: That [that] ye choose as thy spiritual ideal must be able to answer for *every* disturbance, for every hope, for every desire as of a spiritual nature.

Then, as ye meditate upon same, in the mind, ye may find same manifested in thy material experiences; whether this be in the assurances sought as to thy judgment, or in that to enable thee to choose thy activity, or as to the attitude or the activity ye would apply in thy dealings with others.

Reading 3051-6

(Q) *What is the spiritual and mental opportunity I have to demonstrate more perfect vision as related in the physical reading?*

(A) Here these, as we find, should have been corrected rather than allowing a stimulation that has hindered. The demonstration to be made is better cooperation in body, mind and spirit or soul of the entity. Thus, as has been given: Definite decisions in self as to attitudes towards all activities of body, mind and purpose, or the choosing of the ideals. In choosing same for the body, don't trust to the memory, don't trust to the thinking that "this I believe," for you change it often, but write it down: Body. Mind. Soul. Begin with the soul, what is thy ideal? The answer must be within self and of Jesus, the Christ. This, to be sure, is first, last and always.

Then, what is the ideal mentally? This should be: How much meditation, how much application, how much appreciation. These, as we find, may be subdivided or, as changes come each day, rub out and change. What is the mind and the spirit as referred to body ideal? See the body perfect in vision, in thought, in purpose. This is now the purpose of physical, not purpose of the mental. What is the ideal relationship which should exist between self, home, friends, activities in relation to things as well as conditions, as well as experiences? Change these as there is unfoldment in the study of thine own self.

Reading 3249-1

(Q) *What do I do that is wrong?*

(A) Who made us a judge over thee or anyone else? What are thy ideals? Parallel thy activities with thine ideals, not merely in mind but put it on paper so that you may study and take a lesson from same.

Reading 5400-1

(Q) *Am I meeting and fulfilling the purposes for which I am present upon the earth at this time?*

(A) You may meet these. The background is such that it may be done, and the urges are latent and manifest. Do first set the ideal. This isn't the easiest job, either. Not merely saying, "Yes, I believe this," and "Yes, I believe that." Put it upon paper. Draw lines. Put headings: "My spiritual ideal"; what is it? "My mental ideal," as to how the time should be spent in recreation, in study, in work, in social activity, in the various activities necessary for an individual to be well rounded. The ideal way is not "Well, I can't do this," but the ideal way and work towards it. Then, "My ideal physical." What sort of a church would that church be if every member was just like yourself? What would it look like? What sort of home life would there be, if every husband was just like yourself? What is the ideal attitude of a husband, of a father? What is the ideal attitude of a neighbor? of a rancher? of a brother? of those political or social activities? Set them down under each of the three headings. See what they look like. You will rub them out many times, for you will see that they don't fit into your ideal—spiritual ideal—for that can only be one—Jesus, the Christ!

8

●

Practicing the Fruits of the Spirit

Reading 1397-2

But they that show in their daily experiences the seeds of the spirit of truth—patience, long-suffering, gentleness, kindness, even to those that despitefully use them—*they* may then know that He will walk with them.

For man may only sow, God alone may give that increase, that unfoldment, that quickening of the spirit of truth that indeed makes thee free. Free of what? Of the turmoils that arise from disturbing forces that may be manifested in the experiences of a soul as one to another, that seek to glorify or magnify their own selfish desires.

Reading 1404-1

There are many influences and many forces, but only one *spirit* of good. There are many entities in the inter-between, in the borderland, in the shadowland, in the developing along the way; but only one spirit of truth, which is life everlasting!

For, as ye live, as ye make manifestations, ye show in thy daily life who is thy Master, who walketh with thee. Do ye show forth sorrow, do ye show forth grudges, do ye show forth little petty hatreds? These are not—as ye know—of the spirit of truth; they are those things that bring sorrow, sadness, disappointments, shadows of the evil things.

And these flow *only* from the spirit of truth.

Reading 1435–1

Each experience of the entity or soul is as a lesson for the understanding of the fruits of the spirit of truth, that may manifest in a material world; patience, hope, longsuffering, gentleness, kindness, brotherly love. These manifested in the experience bring as the reward the closer relationships with Creative Forces, or God.

For in these we find the manifestations of the spirit of truth, and the associations, the environs, the activities of an entity in any experience in relationship to these bring a workable knowledge in the experience of such an entity.

Reading 1440–1

Or the fruits of the spirit of truth that maketh men *alive* in the consciousness of their relationship to Creative Forces.

For that which is done in the purpose, in the desire for meeting and being one with the ideal—if the ideal is of the spirit of truth—is constructive. But it is not as to what one says, not as to what one may say one believes that counts, but rather what one does *about* that which is the experience day by day.

Reading 1448–2

For only that which is continuous in its creative influence—as Life itself—is everlasting. For that which is *was* and ever will be. Only the mortal or material, or matter, changeth; but the expressions of same prompted by the Spirit of truth live on.

And if there is sought by the entity as much into how Spirit works in and through the emotions of the fellowman (not spirits, but the Spirit of truth), this will not only bring into the experience that as will bring peace and hope and understanding, but will make a growth beyond that as may be even reckoned—in words.

Reading 1456–1

For to find happiness is to find that the Spirit of Truth is *directing* thy footsteps; yes, thy activities; yes, thy very thoughts day by day.

Reading 1463–1

But the still small voice of the consciousness, the awareness of the soul as to its relationships to the Creative Forces, or nature, or nature's expressions, or manifestation of the spirit of truth, and of hope, *must* be in accord with the desires, the purposes, that make for creating the desire to be those things that are in the material experiences of man the evidences of the manifestation of the spirit of truth; as: hope, brotherly love, patience, longsuffering, gentleness, kindness, under and in *every* experience of the activities of an individual soul.

(Q) *Is it cosmically correct that I have further contact, in this present life experience, with this entity, John [. . .]?*

(A) Each may be a prop, a help, one to another. Do not make same a selfish matter, but rather that as may be the helpfulness in each. Give a way or manner of the greater *expressions* of that which may bring the fruits of the spirit of truth as conscious experiences in the lives of others.

Reading 1470–2

Then what is thy ideal as respecting same? Is it set in that which is to be the gratifying of self's purposes as to position, fame, fortune or what not? or is it set in that as ye know, as ye have experienced, that all of these unless directed and prompted by the Spirit of Truth can but come to naught!

But if the ideal is prompted by Truth, no matter what may be the outward appearance, the assurance of filling and fulfilling the purpose for which the entity seeks expression in this experience in every *phase* of its consciousness, it will bring contentment, peace, harmony and the like.

Reading 1472–3

But gathering these, do not condemn. For know, there is only *one* spirit—that is the Spirit of Truth that has growth within same! For if there is the spirit of strife, or the spirit of any activities that bring about contention or turmoils, it takes hold upon those very fires that ye have so *well* put away; yet that keep giving giving—urges that are spoken of, even as He that ye *know*, that the prince of this world is as a raging lion, going about seeking whom he may destroy!

Reading 1493–1

We find such experiences are brought from these innate influences, that are signs or omens or directions; hence have nothing to do other than pointing the way. For while one may be influenced by such signs, the very will is that which makes for the choice itself—which is in its essence the gift of the Creator, that the soul might choose to be one with that which is everlasting; which is and can be only constructive, born of what may be truly said to be the fruits of the spirit of truth itself; as: longsuffering, patience, kindness, brotherly love. Not envying, not making for strife or that which would even make any soul afraid.

Reading 1506–1

The spirit of truth, the spirit of righteousness is ever at the beck and call of those souls that seek to know the will of the Creative Force or God in its dealings with its fellow man.

Reading 1531–1

For keeping the faith is just being one that shows in the experiences with the follow man the things that become the fruits of the spirit; the fruits of the spirit of truth—gentleness, kindness, patience, long–suffering. For these bring their fruits into the hearts and the souls of men. Not that of satisfaction so much as contentment and peace, leaving with the Spirit of Truth the results that are to be accomplished.

Reading 1742–4

(Q) *Should my mental capacities be guided by my spiritual self?*

(A) As has been just indicated, these should be builded *ever* by the spiritual self; for as the mental body *is* aware of the spiritual aptitudes, or the spiritual movements, so does the promise *become* manifest, that "I go to the father, and if I go I will *send* my spirit and he will abide with thee *always*, even unto the end of the earth." So, as the spirit moves thee, so let thy yeas and thy nays be governed by that, and as the activities must be manifest in the material world, so do they *finding expression through* the material mind, but is the motivative forces *of* that mind of the *Spirit*. The *Spirit is* Truth!

(Q) *Should I improve my physical self before seeking a firmer mental hold on myself?*

(A) In seeking to gain a firmer mental *hold* upon self, or seeking to know *self* and self's relationship to the creative forces, will *aid* in *bringing about* a more perfect coordination in the physical being. Let's for the moment, then, visualize that of the spirit of life as it manifests itself through a material body (That's for this body we are speaking of!): Each atom or corpuscle *of* the body is an whole universe within itself, with *all* the attendant elements or sources *of* life about same. So is the taking thought in self alone, as was given, "not able to add one mite or cubit," yet is that thought guided by that which is the motivative forces of life *in God*, and "all power given in Him," then in keeping that consciousness in the abilities of the Son to bring into being all of life that is; hence we may see how those in a material plane may so raise that consciousness to coordinate same with life in its various forms in the earth, as to *magnify* Him the more. Hence the necessities oft that there be *added* in the vibrations *of* the body—*material* body—those of the vibrations of things material, that there be altered, or a coordinating *of* the vibrations for a more *perfect* understanding in a physical, or imaginative, or mental body. The *spirit is* willing, the flesh *is* often weak; yet through understanding of *His* laws, that they all emanate from one source, and what is oft the *best* for coordinating of *one* is *not always* best for another; yet *truth is truth* in Life's activities! So, as the body would know self, and awaken more and more the spiritual aspects *of* the body *in* operation *through* the physical forces *of* the body, this would make more and more alive the vibrations of the physical body. Not in strain, to be sure; forget not, that He oft went aside from His labors—to pray!

Now as we find, there may be help brought to this body, if there can be—under changed environs—the application of that which is the fruit of the spirit of truth, of helpfulness, of gentleness, of kindness, of patience.

Reading 2513-1

Hence from Uranus *and* Neptune we find the delving into mysteries. All forms of psychic influence are of special interest to the entity. Yet oft the entity discredits its *own* experiences. Hold closer to the ideal, that it is not by might nor by power but by the spirit of truth that one accomplishes spiritually—not by entities, but by the spirit of truth—and there is one truth!

As to the appearances in the earth—we find that these have been many. Hence the high emotional nature of the entity. While note all are given here, and while many that have influenced and that may yet influence the entity in this experience may not be indicated at this time, these are chosen to be given here that this may be a helpful influence; thus enabling the entity to see itself and thereby fulfill its purpose, and to be that channel for a living example, that it may be a witness bearing individual for the spirit of truth.

Reading 3051–2

Jealousy, malice, hate, backbiting are not the fruits of the spirit of truth. That which *is* of the spirit of truth is manifested in patience, love, fellowship, kindness. These cost nothing, yet make returns in dividends in peace.

Reading 3377–1

We would minimize the faults, we would magnify the virtues. This should be the policy, the purpose of the entity in its dealings with its fellow man. For as has been indicated in that the body would emulate in the earth "Father, forgive as I forgive." Thus as the entity applies this in the experience and in its dealings with the fellow man, there is the application of that He so oft gave, "As ye do it to the least of my little ones, ye do it unto Me." These should be, then, the tendons, the sinew of the spirit through and in which the entity would apply itself in its efforts to bring help to others, not by might or strength but through the spirit of truth as may be manifested in a word, in a movement, in a smile.

Reading 3388–1

Do not have operations. These would mean a renouncing of that which has builded physically, mentally, and spiritually in the body forces. If there is a continuation there may become distressing conditions through the lower portion of alimentary canal, but the greater help may come through the holding of the correct attitude. Not that there should be a denial of the condition existent, but there should be the continual affirming and the relying on, and the realization of the ability and the power of the Christ Consciousness to make whole. If this is seen and applied in the life in dealing with others, there may come help; not by bragging, not by boasting, not by denying, but rather by edifying all with whom the body comes in contact, and then living day by day in those things and in those ways that the spirit, or seed of the spirit of truth is manifested.

Reading 3395-3

In the application of the tenets or truths it would give to others, the entity will find that what ye gain, what ye attain through the spirit is by the application of the tenets of the spirit of truth. It depends upon the spirit, the purpose, the aim, the desire with which ye act!

Just as the entity has found: certain leaflets, certain tracts seem to have little power, because the entity who subscribed to same did so with the idea of personal gain rather than with the purpose of giving love to those to whom such might appeal. It lost its appeal in the purpose or the spirit with which it was given.

Reading 5749-13

Magnify in the daily life the fruit of the spirit of truth, that all may take hold and make for that activity in their lives; knowing that as ye do it unto the least of thy brethren ye do it to thy Maker.

9

●

The Christ Spirit

Reading 991–1

Christ is not a man! *Jesus* was the man; Christ the messenger; Christ in all ages.

Reading 262–103

Time never was when there was not a Christ and not a Christ mass.

Reading 262–29

(Q) Explain and expand fully the thought that the Christ Spirit, not the man, should be the door, the truth, the way.

(A) That which has been given may be used to illustrate the difference that may be felt by a soul that has become aware of itself, as the Christ, or as Jesus the man became aware of the Spirit of the Father through those experiences of the man as he "went about doing good," and at those periods when there was received those acknowledgements of the Father that he *was* the one who could, *would*, through those activities, become the Savior of man. First, as "in whom I am well pleased"; then as "This is my son; hear ye him!"

In the overcoming, then, He *is* the way, the manner in which individuals may become aware of their souls that are in accord with that as may be one with the spirit of truth; for corruption inherits not eternal life. The Spirit is the true life. Then, as individuals become aware of that ability *in Him* to be the way, so they become the door, as representatives, as agents, as those that present the way; and the door is thus opened; and not to the man but the spirit of self that bears witness with the spirit of truth through Him that overcame the world, thus putting the world under His feet.

So we, as heirs of the kingdom, as brothers one with Him, may enjoy that privilege as He has given to those that hear His voice and put on the whole armor; that we may run the race that is set before us, looking to Him, the author, the giver of light; for in Him ye live and move and *have* their being. Do ye become rebels? Do ye find fault one with another, that are as self heirs to that kingdom? Rather be in that humbleness of spirit, that His will "be done in earth as it is in heaven." Thus do we become the children of the Father, the door to the way, and joint heirs with Him in glory.

Let thy yeas be yea, thy nays be nay. "Let others do as they may, but for me I will serve a *living* God," who has shown in man—*all* men, everywhere—that image of the Creator, in that the soul may grow in grace, in knowledge, in peace, in harmony, in understanding.

Be ye doers of the word; not hearers only. Thus ye become the door that the *Way*, the Christ, the Savior, may enter in; for *He is* the way, the truth, and the light.

Reading 900-227

(Q) *As regards the philosophical phase. I have been asked many times to explain the resurrection of Christ in terms of my concept, embraced in the book I am writing on Spirit Action. Many are the ideas presented to me. Among them that the Christ was taken from the Cross before death and thus appeared as one resurrected. Explain—not so much the emblematical meaning of the resurrection, as to the possibilities of the One Spirit Father being able to manifest itself in physical form of flesh man, even when the entity of that flesh man has gained complete perfection and a complete concept, such as manifested in the Christ, when that flesh man has reached the point of complete dissolution, as it is written in the Scriptures of Christ had reached before resurrection. I ask this question that it may help me to complete the concept and to answer those who put the question to me.*

(A) In this there is presented that which the entity may gain the full concept of, in this one sentence: As in Adam all die, so in Christ all is made alive.

As to the conception of the resurrection, there are many presentations in the physical world of man's concept of same, for, as we find, to understand the resurrection, we must first gain a concept of how the spirit force entered into the body and man became a living soul; for we begin first as this:

The earth and the universe, as related to man, came into being through the *mind—mind—*of the Maker, and, as such, has its same being much as each atomic force multiplies in itself, or, as worlds are seen and being made in the present period, and as same became (earth we are speaking of) an abode for man, man entered as man, through the *mind* of the Maker, see? in the form of flesh *man*; that which carnally might die, decay, become dust, entering into material conditions. The Spirit the gift of God, that man might be One with Him, with the concept of man's creative forces throughout the physical world. Man, in Adam (as a group; not as an individual), entered into the world (for he entered in five places at once, we see—called Adam in one, see?), and as man's concept became to that point wherein man walked not after the ways of the Spirit but after the desires of the flesh *sin* entered—that is, away from the Face of the Maker, see? and death then became man's portion, *spiritually*, see? for the physical death existed from the beginning; for to create one must die, see?

In this, then, there is seen, as the body, in the flesh, of the Christ, became perfect in the flesh, in the world, and the body laid aside on the Cross, in the tomb, the *physical* body moved away, through that as *man* will know as dimensions, and the Spirit able then to take hold of that Being in the way as it enters again into the body, and as it presents itself to the world, to individuals at the time and to man at present.

Reading 900-315

(Q) My one question is: "Am I correct in my deduction that my interview as a disciple to the Master—i.e. was actually an interview with the Lord—'the Redeemer'? Or am I deluding myself, for it would not be the first time my mental consciousness has risen into the very holy of holies—for it has been given that I am one in Israel, whom the Gods have given again the approach even to the Throne—am I correct or

do I go too far, for my interviewer comprehended perfectly my mental needs?"

(A) This is as the direct application of those truths as have been given the entity from time to time, for does not the entity gain that differentiation in the presence of the seeking for the Master and for the pleasures and the interests of making the good impressions in the world? As the impression is felt from within of the presence, and as the impressions are attempted to be made from within of the spiritual understanding that the social position of the physical being has reached to such proportions, just the same, and in just the same status and manner is this true; for the spirit of Christ abroad in the world seeks to be the indwelling factor in the life of those seeking to be like the Master, see?

Reading 900–351

(Q) Night of Oct. 20, or morning of Oct. 21. As predicted [in 900-347 on 10/18/ 27], it came. I seemed to pass through many stages or experience many elements that compose the thoughts—i.e. application of the human mind. There was lust for money, sex lusts and lusts of other kinds—i.e. seeking to gratify various desires of the flesh. There was the desire for travel—or I noted myself seeking to return from a Ft. Wayne trip (we are planning Thanksgiving). Then my mother seemed to kick my brother in the face, which he resented. I put my arm about him and tried to make peace. "See how I have forgotten and forgiven," I said. "Yes, but your trouble is past and now doesn't seem so important," he replied. "I know that is true," I replied, "But come on, be big about it." Then I passed through a dark cellar and up into a lighted room where I beheld Mrs. Berliner (just deceased and for whom or whose soul I had prayed for that night), seated with many others. (I felt her presence a previous afternoon while writing. Following that was a quarrel). She said to me: "I will not have discord in my house. I will not have lack of harmony and trouble there." Then I saw many in the Borderland whose mental application and physical endeavors in the physical had held back their potential development. I asked: "Who will bring them back?" Then a change. I felt and saw as I had once before, when my mind rose into the Holy of Holies—even unto the throne. I beheld Him as a young man this time. He was naked to the waist—yet I saw not below the waist. I asked: "Who is that young man?" "That," I was told, "is Christ." "Who will bring them back?" I asked again. Christ spoke to me directly, saying but two words. He said in reply: "I will."

(A) In this we find there is sufficient matter for study in the many various phases of the entity's endeavors, and the entity's writing, and the entity's mental, physical and moral experience, and the manner as the various phases of this vision present to the entity are those various phases of the development of the entity along the various phases of the truths, lessons, understandings, and the great truth as is the culmination of the thought in that seen in the latter portion of the vision.

In the first we find the fulfillment in time and in manner of lessons as have been presented to the body in this very definite way and manner, and these are all to be studied from that vision of self from within *out*, rather than from out to the within—though we find there is the reasoning from within and the reasoning from without, though we find there are those direct or elemental conditions in the physical presenting various phases of conditions as are experienced through the mental mind. Only gauge all then in its proper sphere, and in the various phases of the studies made by the entity, realizing that all is gained by comparison, and that that in the subconscious or in the cosmic plane is made, as it were, a counterpart of that seen in the material plane, and that there is no condition, element or thing that may not be found patterned in the material or mental consciousness.

In the vision as regarding that of those things that bring about the various forms of desires in the flesh realm, in each instance there is seen the lack of will's force being manifested in the proper direction, or the improper application of will's force as respecting that in the material or mental plane. In the forces as applied in the various phases of self-indulgence, finds its expression in those conditions in which—though loving hands would mete out that diametrically opposite from the ordinary conditions in life. So each becoming in this manner the expression in the comparative degrees of those things experienced and studied in the various developments of the mind.

As is seen in that of travel, or communication—of the various conditions arising from same—these may be seen in all their glory, or in all their blackness—depending upon the attitude of the individual towards that comparison as is being brought forward; yet there is seen in the various conditions—whether pertaining to that in which there is the exercising of the forces from the cosmic plane toward material, or material towards the cosmic forces—that there must be one set as an ensample in the manner, way and force of expressing same. Then the mind rises in its attitude towards that that would bring to all those full forces of the ability to apply that in will in that as opposed, or in the manner of bringing better conditions to the body if will's force applied, making will One with that element that gave to the forces of the world that necessary element to bring all to that throne of grace in which man comes in the closer communication with the Creative forces in the material or cosmic, or the super conscious forces of the universe, and in this relativity of conditions in that He that gave self as the ransom is able to keep that committed unto Him against that day for every individual who puts their trust in Him; for in *Him* comes the way and the light, and the expression from Him that I will go, I will meet, I will give—that rise of expression in the hearts of men, showing to this body that that Spirit is alive in the world today even as on that glorious morn that He broke the bonds of death and rose on the morning light to the Father that gave all to this world that men, through Him, might seek that way of escape from the fleshly lusts that beset in their various ways; for, as is seen, to the entity there is again in this vision that approach to the throne itself, and unto Him is committed that in and through *His name*, the name of the Son, that all may approach to that throne of grace.

Reading 1158–12

What meaneth this? How may it be put into words that one may grasp the meaning of what it means for that Spirit of the Christ—as manifested in Jesus—to be present as it were in a million places, as ye say, at once?

Reading 3418–1

In analyzing the urges latent and manifested that are indicated in the emblems, that seem so foreign one to another—these urges are so at variance at times in the body, in the mind of this entity. And these symbols should remind the entity. Don't feel sorry for self. Know that God is not a respecter of persons, but has a job, yes a work for thee to do in the earth. Build the home, train the young. Aid those who are ill, remembering that all should be done in the Christ-Spirit.

Reading 3706–2

Thus the Law of One as manifested in the way, the truth and the light, which has ever been in the earth in the various periods of activity, is now as the Savior in fact.

Reading 5749–5

Ye, my brethren, in your ignorance and in your zeal have often spoken of that influence in the earth known among men as the record made by those that would influence the activities in the religious or spiritual life of individuals through the ages, as a record of the Son of man as He walked in the earth. Rather would ye listen and harken to those things as He spoke when He made those inferences and illustrations as to how those had closed and did close their ears to what was actually going on about them; yet they knew Him not! He, our Lord and our Master, was the first among those that put on immortality that there might be the opportunity for those forces that had erred in spiritual things; and only through experiencing in a manner whereunto all might be visioned from their greater abilities of manifesting in the various phases, forms and manners as they developed through that ye know as matter, could they come to know how or why or when there was made manifest in any realm spirit that was good and spirit that was in error. For, He gave thee, had ye not *known* the Son ye would *not* be condemned in thine own self. For, condemnation was not in Him, but "ye are condemned already." And in the coming into the influence of those that would open themselves for an understanding might there be the approach to Him. He has come in all ages through those that were the spokesmen to a people in this age, that age, called unto a purpose for the manifestation of that first idea.

Then, He has come in all ages when it has been necessary for the understanding to be centered in a *new* application of the same thought, "God *is* Spirit and seeks such to worship him in spirit and in truth!"

Then, as there is prepared the way by those that have made and do make the channels for the entering in, there may come into the earth those influences that will save, regenerate, resuscitate, *hold*—if you please—the earth in its continued activity toward the proper understanding and proper relationships to that which is the making for the closer relationships to that which is in Him *alone*. Ye have seen it in Adam; ye have heard it in Enoch, ye have had it made known in Melchizedek; Joshua, Joseph, David, and those that made the preparation then for him called Jesus. [GD's note: Essenes, School of Prophets started by Elijah. See Malachi 3 and 4] Ye have seen His Spirit in the leaders in all realms of activity, whether in the isles of the sea, the wilderness, the mountain, or in the various activities of every race, every color, every activity of that which has produced and does produce contention in the minds and hearts of those that dwell in the flesh.

Text of Reading 5749-6

This psychic reading given by Edgar Cayce at the Edmonds' home on Pennsylvania Ave., Norfolk, Va., this 5th day of April, 1936, in accordance with request made by those present.

PRESENT

Edgar Cayce; Gertrude Cayce, Conductor; Gladys Davis, Steno. Minnie Barrett, Esther Wynne, Hannah Miller, Florence & Edith Edmonds, Frances Y. Morrow, Hugh Lynn Cayce, Helen Ellington and Ruth LeNoir. Also Margaret Wilkins, Albert White, Alice Harris, Myrtle Demaio, Nellye Twiddy and Elizabeth Perry.

READING

Time of Reading 4:25 to 5:05 P. M. Eastern Standard Time.

GC: As we approach this Easter season our thoughts turn naturally toward the Biblical accounts of the resurrection of Jesus, the Christ. We seek at this time through this channel information dealing either with a completion of the historical account or interpretation and explanation of the full meaning of the resurrection which will help us to better understand and appreciate it.

EC: Yes. In seeking ye shall find. In the experience of each soul that has named the name of the Christ, this should be a season of rededication of self as being a true messenger of His in and among men.

In seeking, then, to know more of that, as to those here, much may be revealed to those that in their inner selves experienced that material period when *He*, Jesus, walked in the earth.

But for what purpose is this season observed, that caused or called for such a sacrifice that life might be made manifest? Is it not fitting that to those here, to those there in that land, it came at that particular season when life in its manifestations was being demonstrated in the material things about each soul?

How, why, was there the need for there to be a resurrection? Why came He into the earth to die the death, even on the Cross? Has it been, then, the fulfilment of promise, the fulfilment of law, the fulfilment of man's estate? Else why did He put on flesh and come into the earth in the form of man, but to be one with the Father; to show to man *his* (man's) divinity, man's relationship to the Maker; to show man that indeed the Father meant it when He said, "If ye call I will hear. Even though ye be far away, even though ye be covered with sin, if ye be washed in the blood of the lamb ye may come back."

Then, though He were the first of man, the first of the sons of God in spirit, in flesh, it became necessary that He fulfil *all* those associations, those connections that were to wipe away in the experience of man that which separates him from his Maker.

Though man be far afield, then, though he may have erred, there is established that which makes for a closer, closer walk *with* Him, through that one who experienced all those turmoils, strifes, desires, urges that may be the lot of man in the earth. Yet He put on flesh, made *Himself* as naught—even as was promised throughout, to those who walked and talked with God.

In the history, then, of the resurrection as ye have recorded in part, may it be so interpreted that those here, now, that experienced (through that period of their advent) His suffering, may—as Andrew, Martha, Naomi, Loda [?], Elois [?], Phoenix [?], Phoebe [?]—again see those days. Though there were fears from the elements without, from the political powers that made for fears of body and mind, there were the rememberings that *He* had given, "Though ye destroy this temple, in three days it will rise again."

And then as He hung upon the Cross, He called to those that He loved and remembered not only their spiritual purposes but their material lives. For He indeed in suffering the death on the Cross became the whole, the entire way; *the* way, *the* life, *the* understanding, that we who believe on Him may, too, have the everlasting life. For He commit-ted unto those of His brethren not only the care of the spiritual life of the world but the material life of those that were of his own flesh, his own blood. Yea, as He gave his physical blood that doubt and fear might be banished, so he overcame death; not only in the physical body but in the *spirit* body—that it may become as *one* with Him, even as on that resurrection morn—that ye call thy Eastertide.

It is that breaking forth from the tomb, as exemplified in the bulb of the tree of nature itself breaking forth from the sleep that it may rise as He with healing in its very life, to bring all phases of man's experience to His Consciousness—that indeed became then the fulfilling of the law.

On what wise, then, ye ask, did this happen in materiality? Not only was He dead in body, but the soul was separated from that body. As all phases of man in the earth are made manifest, the physical body, the mental body, the soul body became as each dependent upon their own experience. Is it any wonder that the man cried, "My God, my God, *why* hast thou forsaken me?"

Each soul comes to stand as He before that throne of his Maker, with the deeds that have been done in the body, in the mind, presenting the body–spiritual before that throne of mercy, before that throne of the Maker, the Creator, the God.

Yet as He, the Father, hath given to each of you, "I have given my angels charge concerning thee, and they shall bear thee up, and thou shalt not know corruption."

This He demonstrated in the experience of thy Brother, thy Savior, thy Jesus, thy Christ; that would come and dwell in the hearts and lives of you all—if you will but let Him, if you will but invite Him, if you will but open thy own heart, each of you, that He may enter and abide with you.

Hence when those of His loved ones and those of His brethren came on that glad morning when the tidings had come to them, those that stood guard heard a fearful noise and saw a light, and—"the stone has been rolled away!" Then they entered into the garden, and there Mary first saw her *risen* Lord. Then came they of His brethren with the faithful women, those that loved His mother, those that were her companions in sorrow, those that were making preparations that the law might be kept that even there might be no desecration of the ground about His tomb. They, too, of His friends, His loved ones, His brethren, saw the angels.

How, why, took they on form? That there might be implanted into their hearts and souls that *fulfilment* of those promises.

What separates ye from seeing the Glory even of Him that walks with thee oft in the touch of a loving hand, in the voice of those that would comfort and cheer? For He, thy Christ, is oft with thee.

Doubt, fear, unbelief; fear that thou art not worthy!

Open thine eyes and behold the Glory, even of thy Christ present here, now, in thy midst! even as He appeared to them on that day!

What meaneth the story of the Christ, of His resurrection, of the man Jesus that walked in Galilee, without that resurrection morn?

Little, more than that of the man thou thinkest so little of, that though his body-physical touched the bones of Elisha he walked again among men!

Dost thou believe that He has risen? How spoke Thomas? "Until I see, until I have put my hand in his side where I saw water and blood gush forth, until I have handled his body, I will *not* believe."

Ye, too, oft doubt; ye, too, oft fear. Yet He is surely with thee. And when ye at this glad season rededicate thy life, thy body, thy mind to His service, ye—too—may know, as they, that He *lives*—and is at the right hand of God to make intercession for *you*—if ye will believe; if ye will believe that He is, ye may experience. For as many as have named the name, and that do unto their brethren the deeds that bring to them (to you) that closeness, oneness of purpose with Him, may know—ye, too—in body, in mind, that He *lives today*, and will come and receive you unto Himself, that where He is there ye may be also.

Crucify Him not in thy mind nor in thy bodily activities. Be not overcome by those things that are of the earth-earthy. Rather clothe thy body, thy mind, with the thoughts, the deeds, the privileges that His suffering as a man brought to thee, that He indeed might be the first of those that slept, the first of those that came in the flesh, that passed through all those periods of preparation in the flesh, even as thou.

But if ye would put on Him, ye must claim His promises as thine own. And how canst thou claim them unless ye in thine own knowledge, thine own consciousness, *have* done—*do* do from day to day—that thy heart has told and does tell thee is in keeping with what He has promised?

For thy Christ, thy Lord, thy Jesus, is nigh unto thee—just now!

We are through.

Definition of the Christ Spirit

Reading 262–29

(Q) *Please explain clearly the difference between the Christ Consciousness, the Christ Spirit.*

(A) As the difference might be given in that which makes for the birth in the flower, and the flower. The consciousness of the Spirit and the abilities to apply same are the differences in the Christ Consciousness, the Christ Spirit.

As has been given, the devils believe, the devils know, individuals that may be conscious of an activity. Those with the abilities to call upon, to be so unselfish as to allow the Spirit to operate in self's stead, are aware of the Spirit's activity, while those that may be conscious or aware of a truth may not wholly make it their own without that which has been given, "He that would have life must give life;" for *He* thought it not robbery to be equal with the Father, yet of Himself did nothing, "but the Father that worketh in me, through me."

Do thou likewise, that thou may know the consciousness of the Christ Spirit, and experience the operation of that witness, that "My Spirit beareth witness with thy spirit, that the Father may be glorified in you, even as I am glorified in the Father through you. If ye love me keep my commandments, and I will abide with you. I will *not* leave thee comfortless; I will make thee aware of that glory I possessed with the Father before the world was."

In such a manner may individuals become aware of the Christ Consciousness and become one with the operative forces of the Christ Spirit abroad in the earth; for He shall come again, even as ye have seen Him go. *Then* shall the Christ Spirit be manifest in the world, even as the Christ Consciousness may make thee aware of that promised as the Comforter in this material world.

Then, the Christ Consciousness is the Holy Spirit, or that as the promise of His presence made aware of His activity in the earth. The Spirit is as the Christ in action with the Spirit of the Father.

Reading 262–46

(Q) *Please give a definition for, "God so loved the world as to give has only begotten son."*

(A) A beautiful lesson has just been given, and definition. This may suit those seeking this the better.

God, the Father, the first cause, seeking—in the manifestations of self—brought the world, as we (as individuals) observe it about us, into being—*through* love; giving to man, His creation, His creatures, that ability to become one with Him. That son *we* have called the Son of man, the Christ Spirit, the love made manifest in bringing the creature into material being in a plane we have called earth. That son was shown, then, the way, through the love of the Father, and He made manifest that love in giving His earthly, material life for a cause, an ensample, a mediation, a contact with the Father, a mediator for man. Hence in love, through love, God *is* love, in the Christ Consciousness, the Christ Spirit; the Son of man made same manifest in all the experiences through the earth. Hence, as given by the beloved disciple, "God so loved the world as to give His only begotten son, "that we, *through* Him, might have life—God—more abundant. He, though He were the Son, learned obedience through the things which He suffered. He that climbs up any other way than accepting those things that are to be met day by day, even as He, seeks through some other channel. The servant may never be greater than the master. He has given that we may be equal and one with Him, yet through Him, His manifestations, in Him, we live in the earth, we move and have our being.

Reading 254–83

(Q) *Who are the Masters directly in charge? Is Saint Germain—*

(A) (Interrupting) Those that are directed by the Lord of lords, the King of kings, Him that came that ye might be one with the Father.

(Q) *Is Saint Germain among them? Who is Halaliel?*

(A) These are all but messengers of the Most High. Halaliel is the one who from the beginning has been a leader of the heavenly host, who has defied Ariel, who has made the ways that have been heavy—but as the means for the *understanding*. [Isaiah 29?]

(Q) *Is Saint Germain among them?*

(A) When needed.

(Q) *Please give us Thine Identity?*

(A) He that seeks that has not gained control seeks damnation to his own soul! Control thine inner self that *ye* may *know* the true life and light! for he that would name the Name must have become perfect in himself!

(Q) *If Mr. Cayce is a member and a messenger of the Great White Brotherhood, how do the Masters wish him to proceed and should not his activities henceforth be presented as Their Work?*

(A) As the work of the *Master* of masters, that may be presented when in those lines, those accords necessary through the White Brotherhood. This—this—*this*, my friends, even but *limits*; while in Him is the Whole. Would thou make of thyself, of thyselves, a limited means of activity? Would thou seek to be hindered by those things that have made of many contending forces that continue to war one with another even in the air, even in the elemental forces? For He, thy Lord, thy God, hath called thee by name, even as He has given, "Whosoever will drink the cup, even as of my blood, he may indeed be free." While ye labor, let *Him* that is the author, that is the finisher, that *is* the Life, that is the bread of life, that is the blood of life, let *Him* alone be thy guide!

DISCOVER HOW THE EDGAR CAYCE MATERIAL CAN HELP YOU!

The Association for Research and Enlightenment, Inc. (A.R.E.®), was founded in 1931 by Edgar Cayce. Its international headquarters are in Virginia Beach, Virginia, where thousands of visitors come year-round. Many more are helped and inspired by A.R.E.'s local activities in their own hometowns or by contact via mail (and now the Internet!) with A.R.E. headquarters.

People from all walks of life, all around the world, have discovered meaningful and life-transforming insights in the A.R.E. programs and materials, which focus on such areas as personal spirituality, holistic health, dreams, family life, finding your best vocation, reincarnation, ESP, meditation, and soul growth in small-group settings. Call us today at our toll-free number:

1-800-333-4499

or

Explore our electronic visitors center on the
Internet: **http://www.edgarcayce.org.**

We'll be happy to tell you more about how the work of the A.R.E. can help you!

A.R.E.
215 67th Street
Virginia Beach, VA 23451-2061